From
Zero to Hero

From Zero to Hero

How to Master the Art of Selling Cars

J. F. Knott

iUniverse Star
New York Lincoln Shanghai

FROM ZERO TO HERO
How to Master the Art of SELLING CARS

iUniverse Star
an iUniverse, Inc. imprint

iUniverse books may be ordered through booksellers or by contacting:

iUniverse
2021 Pine Lake Road, Suite 100
Lincoln, NE 68512
www.iuniverse.com
1-800-Authors (1-800-288-4677)

Because of the dynamic nature of the Internet, any Web addresses or links contained in this book may have changed since publication and may no longer be valid.

The views expressed in this work are solely those of the author and do not necessarily reflect the views of the publisher, and the publisher hereby disclaims any responsibility for them.

ISBN: 978-1-58348-019-9 (pbk)
ISBN: 978-0-595-89929-6 (ebk)

Printed in the United States of America

In memory of my father
and
for my mother, brother, and wife
for always believing in me.

Contents

Acknowledgments

Thanks to all of the talented, hardworking individuals that I have been fortunate enough to work with over the years. From each of you, I have learned something. Keep up the good work. You make this business great.

"There is no such thing as a self-made man. We are all made up of thousands of others. Everyone who has ever done a kind deed for us or spoken a word of encouragement to us has entered in to the makeup of our character and of our thoughts, as well as our success."

—George Matthew Adams

Scott Hipsky	Merle Simpson
Bill Schaefer	Brandon Schaefer
Jerry Bumbard	Roger Beckley
Dave Matthews	Peggy Drolett
Robert P. Kelly	Jim Allen
Tim Smith	Shannon McCarthy
Tony Kopp	Chris Saraceno
Doug Finwall	Alfred W Cala II
Buddy Vickers	Jimmie Vickers Sr.
Tom Simms	Jim Doyle
Jack Morande	Rich Johnson
Jim Holley	Glenn Wood
Gary Jarek	Charles Algieri
Melissa Sliwinski	Mike Whitty
Bill Page Sr.	Bill Page Jr.
Todd Stewart	Barry Parker
Renard Bergstrom	Tom Devore
Tony Pappas	David G. Alderson
Jim Ahlquist	Robbie Roberts
Nick Laspina	Walter Smith
Donnie Allen	Rex Demoss

"A special thanks goes to Freelove Sommers and Michele Merritt for all of their hard work associated with this book."

Introduction

I started my very first day in the car business by attending a Saturday-morning sales meeting. I listened and watched intently as the general manager, in his expensive Italian suit, silk tie, perfectly pressed white shirt, diamond rings, and solid gold Rolex, stood at the front of the room preaching to all of us about the incredible opportunity we had in the car business. He reminisced about how selling cars had elevated him from a penniless orphan to the top of his profession as a successful, wealthy, automotive salesperson. He bragged that—with no more than a high-school education and his burning desire to become successful—he now had everything he had ever wanted and that the car business had made every one of his dreams, some that he had never even imagined, come true. I could see the pride in his eyes as he told us about the part of his day he enjoyed the most. It occurred in the morning when he pulled out of his driveway and saw the names on his neighbors' mailboxes followed by the abbreviations MD, PhD, and PA, knowing that he too lived in a house as big as, if not bigger than, theirs. There was, however, one big, distinct difference. Under his name on his mailbox, imprinted in large white letters for all of his neighbors to see, was the word "CARSALESMAN."

He considered himself an American rags-to-riches story and wanted everyone around him to know it. No, I wasn't an orphan, and I wasn't penniless when I started selling cars, as he was. I didn't even care to advertise any success I might have in the car business to the people living around me. These were the only ways in which we were dissimilar. I had dreams. I wanted more than a nine-to-five job that would pay the bills. I had a burning desire to be successful.

His speech reaffirmed my belief that the car business would afford me this opportunity. After all, if an orphan with merely a high-school education could live among doctors and lawyers, then anyone could. You don't have to be born on third base to score a homerun selling cars. All you need is the desire to succeed. If you have this desire, then you are one of those for whom I have written this book.

Like many of you, when I began my career in the car business, I was thirsty for knowledge. I searched for classes to make me a better salesperson but to no avail. I bought and read books on the subject of sales but found none that addressed the uniqueness of the automotive-selling process. Little did I realize at the time that most of the knowledge I would gain about selling cars would come to me by way of experience and advice from fellow salespeople; much like urban legends or folk stories, the knowledge I gained and the selling techniques I learned were passed down to me through the words of my more-experienced coworkers.

With each bit of information came a new revelation. And each time I thought I had finally learned everything there was to know about selling cars, I discovered something new. You see, selling cars is different from any other profession; it is not a job that you learn how to perform and then proceed to do. It is a never-ending process of learning new things about yourself and your fellow man. It is about human interaction and relationships, sometimes at their best but frequently at their worst. With this in mind, my purpose for writing this book is not to tell you everything there is to know about selling cars but rather to focus on the most important knowledge I have gained—how to build a strong foundation for a successful career—and to pass on this knowledge in the hope of helping you quickly build the foundation that has taken me years to establish.

"Though no one can go back and make a brand new start, anyone can start from now and make a brand new ending."

—Anonymous

CHAPTER ONE
THE BUSINESS

"Traffic is the life stream of the 20th century. It is a sign of success and prosperity. After all, what is a pedestrian? He is a man who has two cars, one being driven by his wife, the other by one of his children."

—Robert Bradbury

Every day in automobile showrooms across America, the same vicious cycle repeats itself: the car salesman, clutching a worn worksheet, strides across the showroom to his cluttered desk, where a family of four anxiously awaits his return from the manager's office to find out whether they've become the proud owners of a brand-new minivan. The salesman unfolds the ink-covered paper to present the last in a long string of offers and counteroffers, and the family members finally come to the realization that their dreams have not become reality. Not this Saturday. Not at this dealership. The manager did not accept their offer.

With great disappointment, they react out of utter frustration. The father rises to his feet with obvious embarrassment, offering his open hand to the salesman as a sign of gratitude for his time.

"Thanks anyway," snaps the wife. "The price is too high."

"We'll think about it and let you know," adds the husband as he nudges his wife toward the door.

This family's feelings of frustration and loss are only equaled by those of the salesman, who spent the past three hours demonstrating his product, test-driving several vans with the family, having their trade appraised, and trying to build some type of relationship—only to be defeated by a few numbers on a page. What more could he have done? After giving away all of the profit and allowing them a fair trade-in value, he still had no deal.

This scenario has been played out millions of times in automotive showrooms across America since the invention of the automobile. The occurrence has come to be expected not only by the apprehensive potential buyers of automobiles but also by the sellers of these beautifully crafted pieces of machinery.

In my early years working as an automotive-sales profes-sional, I often wondered things like, "Why did this back-and-forth game start, and what purpose does it serve?" and "What has made customers so apprehensive about buying a new car?" I did not find a simple answer to either of these questions. Even questions like, "Who sold the first car?" or for that matter, "Who invented the automobile in the first place?" were difficult questions for which I could not find definitive answers.

Now nearly two decades later, I have come to only one con-clusion, and that is that nothing about the car business is defi-nite. Even a question as simple as the last one seems to elicit conflicting opinions as to the true origin of the modern-day automobile. Some say it all began in 1769 when Nicolas Joseph Cugnot, a French engineer, invented the first self-propelled vehicle, a steam-powered wagon created for use by the French army. Many may point to the fact that both Leonardo da Vinci and Sir Isaac Newton had drawn up plans for motor vehicles hundreds of years prior. Some point to the first U.S. patent obtained in 1789 by Oliver Evans for a self-propelled vehicle.

In fact, thousands of patents could be attributed to the invention of the automobile. However, it was more than a hun-dred years after the United States issued the first patent for one of these machines that J. Frank Duryea drove a self-propelled vehicle on the streets of Springfield, Massachusetts, in Septem-ber 1893 (as reported in the *Springfield Evening Union*); most consider this the official beginning of the American age of the automobile. Two years later, in September 1895, Frank and his brother Charles Duryea established the Duryea Motor Wagon Company in Chicopee, Massachusetts, and by 1896 they had assembled thirteen similar gasoline-powered automobiles in the first known attempt to manufacture and sell automobiles for profit in America. The Duryea brothers advertised their vehicles in magazines and distributed sales brochures outlining some of the benefits of their merchandise, as seen in the following excerpt from their 1895 brochure:

The Duryea Motor Wagon shown on preceding page is believed to be the finest article of its class yet made./It appears much as does the common wagon./It makes little or no noise or odor./It is easily managed by anyone with but little instruction./It is thoroughly practical on all roads over which common traffic passes./It is not dangerous either from fire or explosion.

One might assume, based on the popularity of automobiles in this present day and age, that surely these first manufactured self-propelled vehicles would have been spoken for long before they were even complete and that there may have even been a waiting list for them. That was not the case, however. As with any new and unknown product, people had to be convinced that this new invention would improve their lives. In fact, sales for these first vehicles could be described as sporadic at best. With limited sales and disagreements occurring between the two, the Duryea brothers sold their interests in the Motor Wagon Company in 1898 to the National Motor Carriage Company, and the brothers parted ways. Although each made attempts to start anew and realize their dreams of success in the newly found automobile industry, neither managed to capitalize on the emerging market. Ask any car salesman today who the Duryea brothers were, and your response will most likely be an inquisitive look or the one-word answer, "Who?"

As history has taught us, even though we have a great idea and a new product, the key to our final success ultimately lies in our ability to create a desire and demand for that product among the general public. Charles Duryea may have realized this in 1938 when he said, "Children growing up today will think that Henry Ford invented the automobile," as quoted in the book, *100 Years of American Cars*.

"The man who will use his skill and constructive imagination to see how much he can give for a dollar, instead of how little he can give for a dollar, is bound to succeed."

—Henry Ford

Henry Ford, an engineer by trade, did not ride his first self-propelled vehicle, the Quadricycle, until 1896, the same year the Duryea brothers began to market and sell their version of the automobile. Why then would Henry Ford eclipse the Duryea brothers in the following years? The answer, of course, is that Henry Ford not only had the vision of manufacturing and selling automobiles to the public on a large scale, but he also had the foresight to realize that he must provide a reliable product at a reasonable price and, more importantly, that he must be able to impress upon the people how his machine would improve their lives. This may be the reason that the Ford Motor Company now sells close to four million new vehicles each year.

"There is one rule for the industrialists and that is: Make the best quality of goods possible at the lowest cost possible, paying the highest wages possible."

—Henry Ford

By 2005, a little over a hundred years since the first attempt to build and market cars to the U.S. public, a report posted on www.nada.org conducted by the National Automobile Dealers Association concluded there were 21,640 new car dealerships in operation in the United States directly employing a total of 1,129,600 people. According to this report, on average there are nearly $33,010,000 in new and used vehicle sales per dealership per year contributing to the 230 million vehicles already in use on the roadways of America.

As you can see by these facts, the automobile industry has grown drastically since its inception over a century ago. Much of the growth has been due in part to the efforts of the dedicated sales departments in these dealerships nationwide.

These men and women breathe, eat, and sleep solely for the purpose of selling and delivering automobiles to the American public.

Some reading this book may be new to the car business or may just be considering a career in the automotive sales industry. If this is true, you may be wondering just what a car salesman does for a living and what you will contribute to the world if you become one.

As the old saying goes, "nothing happens until somebody sells something." This statement is true regarding the car business. Consider for a moment that each time a car is sold revenue is created. That is what selling is all about. Most people's jobs consist of doing one of two things. They either provide goods, or they provide services. An automotive salesperson is different. In this job, you do both. However, you don't get paid until you create business and generate revenue. You get paid to sell.

The money generated from the business you create goes to pay the wages of everyone involved in the manufacture, transportation, preparation, and documentation of that vehicle. It may be hard for you to believe, but economic studies listed on www.cargroup.org which were conducted in 2003 by the Center for Automotive Research have shown that automobile sales and manufacturing account directly and indirectly for about 10 percent of the jobs people have in the United States today. Every car you sell helps to pay the salaries of over thirteen million people currently employed in this country. Every one of those peoples' livelihoods is built on the backbone of the revenue you are creating. Hopefully, this fact alone is enough to demonstrate to you how important your choice to be an automotive sales professional is to everyone around you.

"The average American salesman keeps 33 men and women at work—33 people producing the product he sells—and is responsible for the livelihood of 130 people."

—Robert Whitney

Why then, you may ask yourself, do car salespeople, the purveyors of such desirable machines, have such a bad reputation among the people who have grown to love this useful invention? Could it have come from the fast-talking, plaid-jacket-wearing, used-car salesman of days past who has so vividly etched his image in our culture's consciousness or from the experiences the customers have had personally in dealerships in the not-so-distant past? Maybe it is a little of each. Whatever the reason may be, many consumers in the U.S. have come to have a love-hate relationship with their automobiles and the dealerships and salespeople that sell them. With this in mind, it has become ever more important for automotive sales professionals to have a firm understanding of their customers' motivations and actions and, furthermore, to have the knowledge necessary to contend with the roadblocks encountered during the course of a typical sale. In the following chapters, we will look at ways to help you do all of this.

CHAPTER TWO
WORKING YOUR PLAN

"The man who is prepared has his battle half fought."

—Miguel de Cervantes

Different from other highly paid professionals in the world, there are no requirements needed to obtain a job selling cars in the automotive industry today. There isn't a requirement for an advanced level of education. There is no prerequisite for past experience. There is not even a minimum level of training that is considered to be an industry standard. Some may think that all it takes to be a good car salesman is the ability to be a good talker or, worse yet, a good liar. The reality is that both of these could not be further from the truth. The only initial requirement to become a car salesman is the desire to sell cars. However, the steps you take after you are hired will determine whether you become a success at automotive sales, a struggling car salesman, or merely just another nameless face affectionately referred to as a ninety-day wonder after your professional demise.

In 1906, an Italian economist by the name of Vilfredo Pareto proposed a mathematical formula to describe the distribution of wealth and land ownership among his fellow countrymen. He found that 80 percent of the property and wealth was possessed by 20 percent of the people.

What, you may ask, does wealth and land ownership in Italy have to do with the car business? Nothing, actually. However, the observation Mr. Pareto made regarding the majority of something being controlled by the minority is relevant.

This principle, commonly referred to as the 80/20 principle, has been applied to many different aspects in the business world. And even though it may not be precise regarding the hierarchy of automotive sales professionals, there typically is a definitive misdistribution of success among them. This is proven month in and month out as some salespeople consistently out-produce their fellow coworkers by as much as 100 to 200 percent.

So what elements cause certain salespeople to rise above and flourish and others to weaken or perish? Is it an exceptionally positive attitude, dedication to hard work, unbridled enthusiasm, the power to persuade, a well-developed plan, or a little of each? The answer, of course, is a little of each. If misdirected, persuasion, enthusiasm, and a good attitude will only take you so far. A plan will develop you and your talents. A plan will direct and focus your strengths and ensure you are getting the best results possible.

Plan to Succeed

Whether you are starting a business, building a house, selling a car, or even just baking a cake, the success you achieve is based on a solid plan. Studies on www.sba.gov conducted by the Small Business Association have shown that the majority of new businesses in the United States fail within the first year of operation, and many of the remaining ones fail in the subsequent years due in part to the lack of planning. Similar to salespeople, these entrepreneurs may possess a special aptitude for their lines of work; however, they lack vision and planning.

"By failing to prepare you are preparing to fail."

—Benjamin Franklin

Many managers and dealers realize the importance of having a plan and that their successes were founded on their abilities to plan and execute. This is why many dealerships employ an established strategy for handling customers from the minute they arrive at the dealership until they depart with their new vehicle. In a dealership, this plan is referred to as a selling system.

Many of you may be saying, "I already know this," or "This is trivial." If you have sold cars for any amount of time, you should be saying just that, and you should already know the importance of working some type of selling system. How could I possibly write a book about selling cars that does not include this topic? For those of you lacking experience or who haven't worked in a store that operates with some type of a selling system, we need to establish a plan for each customer you encounter. It will be the blueprint upon which you will build each of your sales.

Customer Plan

The remainder of this chapter will lay out a plan for you to follow with your customers from the time you meet them to the moment you have finalized the deal. Later chapters will elaborate on some of the more complicated steps. In this chapter, we will get a brief overview of each.

1. Meet and greet
2. Fact-finding or qualifying
3. Product presentation
4. Demonstration drive
5. Presenting the numbers
   - Negotiating
6. Closing
   - Handling objections

- Finalizing the deal

Meet and Greet

The first step, meeting and greeting, seems too simple to need elaboration. Most of us have been taught from the first day in the car business that you immediately greet someone professionally by introducing yourself, welcoming the customer to the dealership, and shaking his or her hand. Sounds simple enough—one greeting for everybody! You may, however, encounter instances in this business when you can make your customer feel more welcome and relaxed upon arriving at your store if you adjust your approach.

In any other business situation, I would not even suggest that anything less than a professional greeting with a handshake would be appropriate; in fact, our culture demands it. As mentioned earlier, nothing in this business is definite. Even though most new sales personnel are taught to greet all customers the same way, let's examine a few different greetings to see what will best suit our situations.

Types of Greetings

Professional: Welcome to ABC Motors. My name is Joe Auto, and your name?

- Hand outstretched

Casual: Hi, my name is Joe Auto. How can I help you today?

- Give ample space without hand outstretched. Accept their hand if offered.

Anticipatory: Welcome to ABC Motors. My name is Joe Auto. Are you here to look around?

- Give ample space without outstretched hand. Accept their hand if offered.

In order to properly evaluate the different approaches, you must consider the situation in which the greeting is being used, the targeted recipient, and your ultimate goal. First, the situation is a period of first interaction between you and the customer. The targeted recipient may be a person filled with fear, anxiety, and apprehension about the upcoming events or the present situation. The ultimate goal should be nothing more than to make your visitor feel welcome and as comfortable as possible about their visit while you project a positive and professional first impression.

It is hard to discuss the initial interactions between two people without at least giving some note to the link between man's appreciation of his personal space and the comfort and security derived from it. In 1963, Edward T. Hall labeled this study of such relationships *proxemics*. He discovered that there are multiple levels of perceived personal space. The distance allowed in each of the territorial areas is based upon the relationship and circumstances surrounding the participants involved.

Levels of perceived personal space

1. **Public speaking**: The distance observed between an audience and speaker is twelve to twenty-five feet.

2. **Social space**: The distance acceptable between business associates is four to ten feet.

3. **Personal space**: The distance reserved for family and friends and acceptable separation for people in lines at banks and similar places of close interaction is two to four feet.

4. **Intimate space**: The distance reserved for acts such as whispering or embracing normally involving contact is one foot or less.

In theory, most would argue that the professional greeting is the only acceptable way to approach a potential client. After all, you are a professional, and the first impression the buyer has of you means everything. When the exploratory type of professional greeting with extended hand is used, some people visiting your store for the first time may feel a bit apprehensive. They are out of their comfort zone and may even undergo an increase in their level of anxiety due in part to the violation of their personal space that your outstretched hand has presented. Do you want them to feel overwhelmed and as though their personal space has been violated? After all, that is not the goal you set out to accomplish. The uncomfortable feeling that first-time visitors experience may even be the reason why many people reply to such a greeting with, "We are just looking. We will let you know if we have any questions." They are attempting to reclaim their personal space. The last thing on some of your customers' minds is why you did or didn't shake their hand. They are more worried about making a mistake during the car-buying process.

The second and less-formal greeting gives them all the relevant information; you state your name and that you are there to assist them, and you assume they already know the name of the dealership when they pull onto your parking lot. Using a similar greeting that does not seek exact information in addition to a handshake suggests less aggressiveness on your part and may not be as intimidating as the first option. After all, the important thing is that the customer feels welcome and not as though they just entered the first step of a system. This level of casual acknowledgment affords the customer adequate time to acclimate to the situation.

To identify with customers who immediately show outward signs of apprehension, you may want to use the third option: an anticipatory greeting. "Welcome to ABC Motors. Are you here to take a look around?" This immediately starts to relieve some of the customer's preconceived expectations. Isn't that why they are apprehensive in the first place? They have preconceived expectations based on their past experiences or the experiences of others. The anticipatory greeting may even put these negative presumptions to rest so that they may immediately respond with a question or comment regarding what they are seeking or attempting to accomplish. This interaction with you is more conducive to the goal you are trying to achieve.

At this point, you may be wondering how to determine which is the best greeting to use with each person. How would you know unless you had met every person previously? This is actually very simple: you read the body language of the person upon arrival and exit of their vehicle. People will speak to you louder with their actions than they will with their words. You just need to be aware of them.

Example Situations

Use Professional Greeting

Customer exits vehicle, makes eye contact, smiles, and/or heads in your direction

(This customer obviously is open to interaction with you and doesn't have a high level of fear or anxiety about this encounter.)

Use Casual Greeting

Customer exits vehicle, doesn't make eye contact, doesn't head in your direction, or stays stationary

(This customer may be exhibiting signs of confusion, fear, or anxiety in regard to the present situation.)

Use of Anticipatory Greeting

Customer exits vehicle with eyes averted and immediately heads in opposite direction without acknowledging you

(This customer shows immediate signs of fear or anxiety about the upcoming encounter and should be approached cautiously.)

By understanding these differences in your customers and approaching them accordingly, you will find that you are not only alleviating tension for the customer but you are also making your job easier.

After the initial meeting, anyone else in the dealership should use a customary, professional greeting—that is, after the customer acclimates to his or her surroundings and becomes more at ease with the situation and the environment.

"Of all the things you wear, your expression is the most important."

—Janet Lane

Qualifying and Fact-Finding

"Qualifying and fact-finding" is the process you will use to determine the requirements your customer has regarding their new vehicle purchase. It is the process you will use to determine your customer's wants and needs. Many customers today know exactly what they are looking for before they arrive at your store, and they will be happy to inform you as soon as the words "Can I help you?" roll off your tongue. Some customers will tell you exactly what they want and may even go as far as to tell you how they want to buy it right upfront. Conversely, a large number of customers that arrive at your dealership have not kept up with the new models and options that are available. They simply want to "look around."

This is the point when many salespeople have been taught to ask qualifying questions. What type of vehicle are you looking for? Do you want two doors or four? Do you want power windows and power locks? Do you want an automatic or a five speed? Do you want leather or cloth? How about the navigation system? To the customer who is only interested in looking around, this questioning may seem like an interrogation of sorts, and that is exactly what some salespeople have made it. Each time you require your customers to answer a question, you are requiring them to make a decision. Put yourself in their place. Would you want someone peppering you with questions requiring you to think and make decisions the minute you walk into a store? Remember, if your customers want to look around at the vehicles that are available, take that as a positive sign that they are interested in seeing your products.

Imagine for a moment that you go shopping for something as simple as a new suit. Suppose you haven't purchased a new

suit in a while and that some of the styles have changed since you last purchased one. Would you feel comfortable with a salesperson who, when you express a desire to look around the store, interrogates you with questions such as, "Do you want single or double breasted? Do you want two, three, or four buttons? What color? Stripes? Do you want cuffs or not? Pleated? Single or double pleated?"

This rattling off of questions may create an uncomfortable feeling for you. After all, you just want to look around at your options. This whole situation may even make you feel rushed or pressured. You haven't even seen suits with three and four buttons, so how would you know? All you know is that you want a new suit.

Let's take it one step further. What if you *had* answered those questions and then saw something contrary to your expressed desires? Would you then go against what you just told the salesperson? You may. However, our culture in America does not highly regard people who are indecisive or who change their minds about things frequently. We have even come up with derogatory names for people who change their mind too frequently. We may call them wishy-washy or say that they can't make up their mind and may even go so far as to label them a liar because their actions don't match their spoken words. Because of this, you should always remember that if you ask your customer questions that are too specific then you might be limiting their options.

Here is another issue associated with the questioning approach. What if you were shown exactly what you had stated you were looking for, but after seeing the price you determined that you couldn't afford it? Would you tell the salesperson that the suit was more than you could afford? Doubtful. You would probably lie and say you need to think about it and that you will be back, when in reality you are just going to go to another store and find a less expensive suit.

I am not saying that you should not ask questions. However, I do feel it is important to learn to ask the right questions. Do not immediately interrogate your customers about the exact options they must have the minute they tell you their names or show lack of direction. Ask open-ended questions that invite them to give more than yes or no answers, nonspecific questions that leave customers open to explore other options. Remember, your customers may be looking for a change—something different, something new to them. This desire for something new and different may be what brings them into your store in the first place. Dissatisfaction with their current situations has motivated them enough to look for a satisfactory solution.

"All purchases are born of dissatisfaction. No purchase of any product anywhere—impulse or deliberation—is ever made unless the purchaser is first dissatisfied in his present state."

—William M. Bryngelson

Open-Ended Questions
Example Interaction One

Salesperson: Welcome to ABC Motors. My name is Joe Auto, and your names?

Customer: My name is Scott, and this is my wife, Katie. But we are just looking today.

Salesperson: Great. We here at ABC Motors encourage you to look at all of your options. We have cars, trucks, vans, and SUVs. Which would you like to begin looking at first?

Customer: Well, we have a minivan now, but we were thinking about getting an SUV this time.

Salesperson: To the left are our new vehicles, and to the right are the previously owned. Where would you like to begin?

Customer: I don't buy new cars. I like to find something that is a year or two old with low miles that someone else has already taken the depreciation on. That way I get more options for my money.

- **Start walking in the direction of the used SUVs.**

Salesperson: Great. What would you consider to be the two or three most important features of the new car you'll be buying?

Customer: (Husband) I am very concerned about the safety of a vehicle. My wife hauls our kids and their friends around a lot, and I want to make sure they are safe in case she ever gets into an accident.

Customer: (Wife) Plus it has to get good gas mileage. With the price of gas these days, I don't want a gas guzzler. Between taking the kids to and from school and soccer practice and over to their friends' houses, I drive so much that I feel like a taxicab driver sometimes.

Example Interaction Two

Salesperson: Welcome to ABC Motors. My name is Joe Auto, and your names?

Customer: My name is John, and this is my wife, Patty. But we are just looking today.

Salesperson: Great. We here at ABC Motors encourage you to look at all of your options. We have cars, trucks, vans, and SUVs. Which would you like to begin looking at first?

Customer: The trucks.

Salesperson: Great. Which one of you will be the primary driver of the new vehicle?

Customer: I will. My wife already has an SUV that we use as the family vehicle.

Salesperson: To the left are our new vehicles, and to the right are previously owned vehicles. Which would you like to look at first?

Customer: We never buy used. I don't want to buy someone else's problem.

- **Start walking in the direction of the new trucks.**

Salesperson: I can understand that. Will you be using this vehicle primarily for personal or business use?

Customer: This vehicle is for work only. I own a plumbing company, and I have a lot of tools and supplies that I have to haul around from job to job. My trailer weighs seven thousand pounds when fully loaded, and my old truck was having trouble pulling it. Plus, I need an extended cab now to put my important things in.

Salesperson: So you own a plumbing company. That's great. Will anyone be driving the vehicle when you aren't?

Customer: (Laughs) No one. I am giving my guys, my employees, my old truck, and I will be driving the new one.

At this point, there still may be a little more information that you are going to need. However, you have not boxed your customer into a situation in which they feel uncomfortable. You will find that customers will interact with you more openly if they are given the chance. They will inquire about the options that are important to them. You may even find that as soon as they walk up to a vehicle they are interested in that they will ask you questions regarding it. Furthermore, the answers you will get by using these open-ended questions will benefit you and the sales process in multiple ways.

Benefits of Open-Ended Questions

- Give you the necessary information you need to lead your customers to the type of vehicles they are interested in

- Allow the customers to feel as though they can explore other options if necessary

- Encourage conversation between you and the customers, helping you to discover not only what they want but also why they need it

- When customers are encouraged to talk about themselves, they feel as though you are interested in them and their lives more so than if you simply ask for the list of options they require

"What we see depends mainly on what we look for."

—John Lubbock

This last benefit in the list above can be one of the biggest advantages you gain by using open-ended questions. People like to talk about themselves, their families, their jobs, and their likes and dislikes. This is evident by the fact that they put bumper stickers on their cars such as "Ask me about my grandchildren," "Honk if You Like Peanut Butter," and "My Child is an Honor Student at ABC Middle School" and license-plate frames that indicate they would rather be skiing, fishing, hunting, shopping, or whatever it is that interests them.

Remember that one of the things that distinguishes humans from animals is their desire to feel important. You are not making your customers feel important when you rattle off a series of questions regarding specific options on the vehicle they wish to purchase. You are making them feel like they are nameless faces in step two of the sales process.

Once you get to know people for who they are, it is not difficult to know their wants and needs. It is easier to know what they want when you know them in a personal manner rather than as just a list of options they want. It is easier because you know why they need these options. It may even afford you the insight to suggest a vehicle they hadn't even considered. You may be able to solve their problems with their dissatisfactions better than they themselves thought they could. You have to know your customers first.

"You must look into people, as well as at them."

—Lord Chesterfield

The advantage gained by learning the customers' wants and needs while learning about them as people and about what is important in their lives became crystal clear to me about six months after I began selling cars.

One Saturday I met a couple interested in buying a sport-utility vehicle. Within a couple of hours, we had selected a vehicle for them, test-driven it, and negotiated numbers. (It is important to note that they were very concerned about money and not willing to go over their predetermined budget for anything in the world, or so I thought.) Now all that was left was a wait to get into the finance office. As we sat at my desk, I (under specific direction from my manager not to discuss any more aspects of the deal) began to talk to them about their lives. At one point in the conversation, they shared with me the fact that they were soon going to be remodeling their house and needed the extra room in a vehicle that the SUV they were purchasing would afford them. At that point, the wife pointed to a luxury car sitting in the middle of the showroom floor and commented, "That is the car we would really like to own, but we need more space so we are buying the SUV." Little did she realize that the car to which she was referring, a Saab 900 Turbo (with a $1000 bonus for the salesperson who sold it), actually had more usable space than the Toyota they were about to take delivery of.

At this point, I decided to excuse myself from the table to confer with the desk manager. Upon my return, I found that my customers had gotten up to get a closer look at the car they had been ogling from afar. Armed with facts I obtained at the sales desk, I informed them that not only did the Saab 900 have more usable space (with the seats folded down) but it also had a lower point of entry for loading and unloading. Needless to say, I could see their eyes light up and the gears move in their heads, and I concluded by telling them that the payment would be only about fifty dollars more per month than the SUV they were about to buy.

As we sat down to rewrite the paperwork on their new Saab 900 Turbo (for fifty dollars a month more than they were willing to pay for the SUV), I learned two valuable lessons.

Lesson One

Once you learn who your people are, it is easy to determine what they want and need.

Lesson Two

People are willing to pay extra for what they want, but not always for what they need.

We will examine further in chapter five the benefits of getting to know your customers. For now, we will move on to the next step.

Product Presentation

"Confidence and enthusiasm are the greatest sales producers in any kind of economy. Have confidence in your products and the house backing them, have enthusiasm for your job, call on your trade regularly and consistently, treat your trade courteously, and you will find that your customers will not have to be sold—they will be glad to buy."

—O. B. Smith

This by far is usually regarded as the easiest part of a salesperson's job, and, as such, many overlook its importance. Whether or not your potential customer has come to you with previous knowledge of the vehicle he or she is considering purchasing, it is important for you to share the vehicle's options, as well as the manner in which the customer will benefit by having them. Additionally, this is the first opportunity you have to demonstrate your competence and begin to instill confidence in the customer that you are a true professional. Some customers may not even be as impressed by all the features and benefits as they are by the fact that they are actually dealing with a highly trained, knowledgeable salesperson who shows enthusiasm for their product.

"Knowledge is power, but enthusiasm pulls the switch."

—Ivern Ball

Once the customer has displayed interest in a vehicle, you should pull it out of the spot it is parked in and preferably take it to an area that will encourage your customer's uninterrupted attention, as well as yours. This will allow you to separate the car from others parked around it, making the process of selection less confusing for the customer.

It is always advisable to try to gear your presentations to the interests of the consumer presently in front of you. Some consumers may be primarily interested in ride and comfort, and some may only care about gas mileage or safety. This is when it is beneficial to have asked what two or three things are most important during the qualifying phase. Now you can tailor your presentation to what the customer has deemed most important. Proceed by sharing the features and benefits that the customer will be receiving. Make sure to emphasize the features of the car that will meet the customer's most important needs. Be careful not to get into too lengthy a dissertation, or you will run the risk of losing your customer's attention. As a general rule, you will want to keep your presentation around seven to ten minutes in length. This is not the opportunity for you to show off everything you know about the vehicle. Customers are more concerned that the information you share with them applies to their needs.

Try to keep in mind that it is always advisable to refrain from using technical terms when describing the features of your product, and if you need to use them make sure to define the meaning for the customer in simple layman's terms. Some people may not know that "ABS" stands for "anti-lock braking system." To further demonstrate the importance of this point, think back to a time when you where shopping for something and thought you had some knowledge of the product and its workings. This may have happened when you bought your first home, boat, or computer. You may have been totally confused by a salesperson who spoke in technological lingo. The last thing you wanted to do was look like you were unknowledgeable by asking a question he assumed you already knew the answer to. This may have caused you to decide that you needed to take a step back from the situation and do some more research or reexamine your needs. In reality, all you needed was a little clarification on an aspect that the salesperson inadvertently spoke of in a manner that was too technical for your level of knowledge.

Five Important Rules for a Successful Presentation

- Be enthusiastic; it is contagious.

- Take the vehicle to a location where you will not be interrupted.

- Tailor your presentation to the two or three things your customer finds to be the most important aspects of the vehicle in which he or she is interested.

- Keep your presentation brief and interesting—seven to ten minutes preferably.

- Refrain from using language that is too technical for your consumer, and, if necessary, be sure to define terms that are not widely known.

Demonstration Drive

The demonstration drive is that portion of time you spend with the customer when they get their first interaction with your product. It is not the time for you to continue your sales presentation on features and benefits. It is a time when you should allow the customer to experience the ride and feel of his or her new vehicle. Yes, his or her new vehicle. More than ever, this is the time when more people will imagine themselves as the owners of the vehicle. This is the point when they take mental ownership of it. So why is this segment of the sales process quite frequently downplayed by sales personnel? Many salespeople get to the point where they don't even go with the customer on the test drive. This is not a recommended practice since many customers are not as familiar with the vehicles as you, and they may have questions that you can easily answer for them. What happens if they hear a noise that is unfamiliar to them? Do they return to your store with the car and, rather than mention the problem, give a prepared excuse as to why they must leave? It could have been something as simple as a squeaking in the brakes that may occur when disc brakes get a thin film of rust on them after being exposed to a moist atmosphere without being driven for a short period of time. People unfamiliar with the occurrence may suspect that a brand new vehicle has problems with the brakes, and there aren't many people who want to buy a problem vehicle.

"What you do when you don't have to, determines what you will be when you can no longer help it."

—Rudyard Kipling

The actual process of driving the vehicle that the customer is thinking of buying is, in reality, one of the pivotal points to selling the vehicle. This is not to say that a person will never buy a vehicle without having driven it first. However, it definitely helps to decrease the likelihood that the customer will decide not to buy based upon anything other than the financial matters involving the purchase.

The three most important things you can do as a salesperson to help improve the customer's experience when driving the vehicle are:

- Make certain they are familiar with the most important controls of the vehicle before they begin to drive.

- Have a preplanned route for test-drives that consists mainly of right-hand turns.

- Use this opportunity to allow the customer to experience the ride of the vehicle, not as a time to continue your presentation.

Presenting the Numbers—Negotiating Price

For buyers, the negotiating process is probably the greatest source of tension and animosity toward the automotive business. However, it is far from being a secret. Saying that it is would imply that it's not known or understood by many. In reality, due in part to a variety of books written for consumers on the subject and the popularity of the Internet, today's buyers have more resources to learn the process used by dealerships to negotiate car deals and are more educated in the process than ever.

Among automotive-sales professionals, there is no other aspect of the selling business that is more hotly debated than the proper way to present figures to a customer and the negotiation of a deal. No two dealerships negotiate exactly the same. Some dealerships have a defined negotiating system within their selling system and require that their salespeople follow a script for the presentation of the numbers. Although many dealerships employ similar techniques when presenting and negotiating figures with a customer, the overall process itself becomes as diverse as the personalities of those participating in the experience. Some dealerships don't even follow a system for negotiating deals.

Many dealerships today employ some variation of a manager-controlled negotiating system and have for decades. Although well-known and disliked by the public, this system still affords management the ability to control the negotiations of a deal with consumers by engaging them in a process of offers and counteroffers, creating an advantage for the dealership. In reality, it is not much different than the process of buying a home. On the one side, you have a potential buyer and an agent as an intermediary, and on the other side you have a seller. The seller has a price that he is asking for his property. The agent solicits a committed offer from an interested party and presents it to the seller. If the seller is not agreeable to the proposal, then they may make a counteroffer in return, and the process goes back and forth until one party agrees to the price or ceases to make any more offers.

Typically, the dealership where you work will employ one of two different formats for conducting this system of desk-controlled negotiations or no system at all. If you are at a dealership using one of the two types of desk-controlled negotiations, you will present to your customer the initial numbers given to you by the manager on either a worksheet or a buyer's order. Although there are variations, most dealerships use a worksheet commonly referred to as a "four square." This is due in part to the division of the paper into four separate sections. One section of the worksheet may contain the vehicle-pricing information, the second may contain the trade-value information, the third may contain a down payment amount, and the fourth may contain payment options. Notice that I said "may" for each section. All dealerships modify the amount and type of information they give the customer. Some may use a large down payment with short-term financing as an option for the customer to consider. Some may use long-term financing with very little down payment to make the offer more appealing, and others may not even use all of the sections on the worksheet. Whatever arrangement a dealership uses, its intent is to use a form that gives the customer enough information to make a committed offer to purchase the vehicle. This is the key objective to presenting the initial set of numbers in any dealership: get a committed offer. The process of obtaining the commitment to purchase upon agreement of figures is the most important aspect of the sales process. Without a commitment, you could present numbers all day, and the customer would let you run back and forth until the numbers were satisfactorily low or until deciding that you have provided enough information and then leave without making the purchase.

The commitment to purchase a vehicle at a dealership may consist of as little as a customer signing his or her name on his or her offer with an understanding that he or she will purchase the vehicle upon approval of the deal, or it may consist of as much as a monetary deposit for the amount of the down payment. This commitment type varies from store to store. Interestingly, this may also be the very event that makes the negotiating process so stressful for people. They are asked to make a decision. This is not much different than the process of making an offer on property. Real estate purchases require that a person put down "good-faith money" (a nonrefundable deposit) to make an offer on property. The deposit is a representation of the buyer's commitment to follow through with his or her offer if the selling party accepts it.

If a dealership wants to use a more assumptive approach to presenting the first set of numbers, they will use a purchase order in place of the four-square worksheet. The numbers may be presented in much the same way as the four square; however, a more assumptive approach is being implied to the customer. Overall, the results expected with the use of a purchase order, a committed offer, or an offer to buy remain much the same as with the use of the four square.

Some dealerships may use no system at all to negotiate deals. They may even give the sales personnel authority to negotiate their own deals without the use of a sales desk as a controlling factor. This only works effectively if the sales personnel involved are experienced and have a high level of competence.

With no universally accepted method for this phase of the selling process, you will find a need to tailor your presentation to conform to the procedures of the dealership where you are employed. We will more closely examine the negotiation process in chapters nine and ten.

Closing the Deal

In every sales process, there comes a point when one of the participating parties closes the deal. Sometimes the salesperson closes the customer and a vehicle is sold, but more often than not the customer is the party who closes the deal successfully. Typically, salespeople that can successfully close 25 percent of their deals are considered to be successful. Be that as it may, this would mean that 75 percent of the time the customer is closing the salesperson with one of many objections as to why they can't buy.

A commonly held philosophy in the automotive business is that the more effort you put into selling the customer, the less effort you will need to put into closing the deal. It is not until this point in a sale that you begin to realize the impact that the other steps of the process have on the final outcome. If you are not able to make your customers comfortable with their surroundings, if they are not sold on your product and the dealership, or if the numbers just aren't quite right for them, then you may find yourself in the long process of reselling, renegotiating, and overcoming objections. This is another example of how the 80/20 principle works. If you spend 80 percent of your time selling, then you will spend 20 percent of your time closing. However, if you spend only 20 percent of your time selling, then you may find 80 percent of your time is spent closing your sales.

Many in sales believe that if they just become better closers, then they will sell more vehicles, and this may be true to a certain point. But just the same, they must also realize that if they become better at selling, they will become better at closing. It is essential to realize the importance of the groundwork laid throughout the sales process and how it relates to the final step of consummating a deal. If your presentation is lacking, you may find yourself reselling the customer on the benefits of your product. If you did not properly qualify your customer, you may find that he or she is not happy with the selected vehicle, and you will be forced to select a vehicle that is more suited to his or her needs. If you fail to test-drive the vehicle with a customer, you may find yourself getting up from the negotiating table to go test-drive a vehicle. If you didn't get a commitment when you accepted the customer's offer, you will find yourself trying to get him or her to commit to buying your vehicle and maybe even renegotiating the numbers. It is easy to identify when one of the steps in your system is lacking: the customer will simply say, "I need to think about it." If you have done everything right, you will hear this less often. Invest the time to do things right the first time, and you will find yourself dealing with fewer objections later in the negotiating phase of the sales process.

Once you have a plan, it is important for you to develop yourself optimally to afford yourself every opportunity for achievement with that plan. As mentioned earlier, more than one factor contributes to your ultimate success in the car business. Without a great attitude and an abundance of enthusiasm for what you do, it is unlikely that you will be successful, regardless of your plan. In the next two chapters, we will examine the influence these two factors have on you and your level of performance.

CHAPTER THREE

THE IMPORTANCE OF ATTITUDE

"Nothing can stop the man with the right mental attitude from achieving his goal; nothing on earth can help the man with the wrong mental attitude."

—Thomas Jefferson

Have you ever had one of those days when nothing seemed to go right? The day didn't start off on the right foot, and with each bit of bad news it went spiraling out of your control even more. You just couldn't say the right words to any of your customers, and everything you did worked against you. You may have simply just written it off in your mind as a bad day.

On the other hand, you have probably had days when you felt as though you were made of steel. Your day started off right. You were happy; you had plenty of energy; and everyone you talked to wanted to buy from you. You were a walking, talking, selling titan. You were in the zone. At the end of the day you may have asked yourself, "Why can't every day be this good?"

If you can identify with this then maybe you are allowing your attitude to be determined by your environment. Unfortunately, if this is true then you are permitting your environment to decide your ultimate fate. You are not alone; many of the salespeople I have met and worked with allow their attitudes to be governed by the circumstances they encounter. Some people only have a positive attitude when everything is going well around them. When the waters are calm, it is smooth sailing, but when the waves get rough they lose control of their ships. These same people allow their attitudes to get tossed in any direction like a ship in a storm at sea being battered about and governed more by the waves than by their own actions. These descriptions bring to mind an expression that a manager remarked to me early in my career. He stated, "Anyone can pilot a ship through calm waters. It takes a real captain to guide a ship through a storm." This proclamation is true regarding you and the attitude you maintain on a daily basis. Each and every day, you choose the type of attitude you face life with— that is, if you step up to the wheel and take control of your ship.

Stop letting the winds and waves of chance determine your destiny. Steer your ship to success.

"The meaning of things lies not in the things themselves, but in our attitude towards them."

—Antoine de Saint-Exupery

As an automotive-sales professional, a positive attitude is not optional. Actually, it is your job to present yourself, your dealership, your product, and the deal you are offering to your customer in the most positive, most favorable light possible. The top performers know this and are able to summon on demand the most suitable state of mind when it will benefit them the most. They can consistently maintain a positive attitude or just "turn it on" in an instant. You too can learn to control your attitude if you understand the factors that influence it.

In this chapter we will examine the effect our attitude has on the situations we encounter on a daily basis, the things that influence our attitude toward these situations, and, better yet, the actions we can take to improve our attitude.

Attitude Is Determined by Perception

Whenever the subject of attitude comes to mind, I cannot help but be reminded of a joke I heard many years ago.

A mother and father took their twin boys, Kyle and Tyler, to see a psychiatrist. It seemed that Kyle was negative about everything that occurred, whether it was good or bad, and Tyler viewed the world as a perfect place where nothing could go wrong. After consulting with the family, the doctor found it hard to believe that twin boys could have such drastically different perceptions of the world surrounding them, so he proposed an experiment.

He told the parents, "On Christmas morning I want you to give Kyle every toy he could possibly want. For Tyler, I want you to give him nothing more than a bucket of horse manure. I will come over and observe their behavior, and maybe I can help make some sense out of this."

Christmas morning arrived, and, as planned, Kyle was given every toy imaginable, and Tyler was given nothing more than the bucket of manure. When the doctor arrived, he noticed Kyle sitting on the living room floor in front of his new train set with a distraught look on his face.

"How is your Christmas going?" asked the doctor of Kyle.

"Not so good," responded Kyle. "Every time I put my train on the track, it just falls off. Nothing ever works right for me."

Next, the doctor decided to check on Tyler and see how he was responding to the gift he had received.

At that moment, Tyler came running in from the backyard, carrying his bucket.

The doctor stopped him and asked, "Tyler, how is your Christmas going?"

"Great," responds Tyler. "I got a new pony. All I need to do is figure out where my parents hid it."

This joke drives home the first point that I want you to realize about your attitude. Your attitude is merely the perception you have about the situations and circumstances that surround you. Does the way you perceive each situation change the conditions you are facing? No, but it does change the way you respond to them. Like a self-fulfilling prophecy, your attitude and your resulting actions ultimately determine the outcome.

"Sometimes we are limited more by attitude than by opportunities."

—Unknown

A case in point is how two salespeople facing the same conditions can end up with completely opposite results. For example, consider the salesperson who calls the bank for a trade payoff amount only to find that his customer owes eight thousand dollars more on the vehicle than it has been appraised for. He immediately responds by thinking, "Why do I always get customers that are eight thousand dollars upside down?" and hangs his head in disgust as he proceeds to tell his customer that he or she is "buried" or "upside down" and needs to pay on the vehicle for a little while longer and get caught up. Even after his customer has left, the salesperson may be so convinced that this person is so "sale proof" that he walks around the showroom and asks any available fellow salesperson that will lend an ear why he can't get a customer that he can make money on.

On the other hand, a salesperson with a positive attitude knows that with the right plan and a little creativity they can put a deal together. After all, negative equity is not impossible to overcome, and the customer is willing to buy now. With the combination of the right vehicle (perhaps a used, current-model-year vehicle with no book value), a little money down (as little as the customer's next payment), and great salesmanship, this salesman will not only sell another vehicle, but he will make money doing it. Always remember that hidden inside every challenge is an opportunity.

"Ability is what you're capable of doing. Motivation determines what you do. Attitude determines how well you do it."

—Lou Holtz

The Focus Factor

So what is the difference between these two salespeople? Of course, the answer is the attitude each has toward the deal. The first perceives the situation to be hopeless, and the second perceives an opportunity. But why do these two salespeople have different perceptions of the deal they are facing? Why does one fail to make a deal while the other not only sells a car but also manages to make money in the process? The answer is that each of the salespeople focuses on different aspects of the deal. One focuses on the problems, and the other focuses on the possible solutions.

Like the two salespeople described above, what you focus on will determine your perception of the situation you encounter. One's perception becomes reality. If you focus on the problem, then your reality will be that you have a problem—not a solution, but just a problem you want to get rid of. In the same situation, your reality, another person's reality, and the true reality may all be different. Does another person's version matter to you? No. Why? Because your reality is what you perceive to be the truth, and once you believe it you will act on it accordingly. Herein lays the secret to managing your attitude on a consistent basis. By controlling your focus, you will change your perception of the situations you encounter, and as a result you will have a better attitude toward them. It is much easier to have a positive attitude when you see solutions rather than problems.

The first salesperson in our example focused on his version of the truth that his customer was "sale proof." For this reason, he had a negative attitude toward the deal and acted accordingly by dismissing his customer and not exploring possible solutions. He got rid of his problem.

The second salesperson's version of reality was that there was a solution to his customer's situation, and his resulting truth was that he had an opportunity to sell another car. He focused on finding solutions. He focused on what he could do to sell a car. Because of this, he found a solution and, in the end, was triumphant.

"Human beings, by changing the inner attitudes of their minds, can change the outer aspects of their lives."

—William James

Controlling Our Focus/Internal Influences

By learning to control what you focus on in life, you can improve your attitude toward the situations you face and, as a result, will find more productive resolutions to them. "But how do I control my focus?" you might ask. This is actually the easy part if you know which tools to use. We all have them. Some of you may not realize them, or you may just be using the wrong ones. The tools that I am referring to are the questions we ask ourselves on a continual basis. Whenever we are confronted with a situation, our internal dialogue kicks in. This is the pro cess by which our mind asks us questions and then responds with answers. We all do it. It is what we use to adjust our focus. It is how our mind thinks, rationalizes, and makes decisions. Become more conscious of this process; learn to control it by asking yourself better questions, and you will get better answers. You will discover solutions.

For instance, take the questions each of the salespeople in our previous example asked themselves. The first salesperson asked himself questions such as, "Why do I always get customers that are eight thousand dollars upside down?" or "Why can't I get someone I can make money on?" These questions focused his mind on the problem and consumed it in such a way that he never even considered a possible solution. These questions focused him in a direction that led him to respond with a negative outlook or attitude toward the situation. Many times these questions have such a powerful effect they don't even need to be answered in order to do damage. The questions alone blind the person asking them to the possible solutions and, furthermore, poison one's attitude.

The second salesman, on the other hand, asked himself questions such as, "What can I do to make this deal happen?" or "What can I do to sell this person a car?" He asked himself questions that focused on solutions. This directed his focus in a more optimistic, positive direction and resulted in answers that ultimately led to accomplishment.

Whether the questions you ask yourself on a daily basis are positive or are what I refer to as "pity-party" questions, they are the tools your mind uses to give your focus an adjustment. They will determine the direction in which you head and will ultimately decide whether you are a success or a failure.

Some of you may have already trained your thought process to seek better answers by asking better questions. Some of you ask yourselves all of the wrong questions and focus on the problems, not the solutions, thereby poisoning your attitude. Let's take a look at some of the focus-killing questions you may be asking and find better alternatives.

"Pity-Party" Questions

- "Why are all of my customers eight thousand dollars upside down?"

- "Why can't I get a buyer?"

- "Why is traffic so slow?"

- "Why can't I make a big gross on a deal like the other salesmen?"

You may have noticed that most of the "pity-party" questions that detour your focus and feed a negative attitude begin with the word "why." That is unless you have gotten to the point at which you have asked some of these questions too frequently. So frequently in fact, that you believe them to be so undeniably truthful of the situations you encounter that you have transformed them into declarations and engrained them into your belief system. Once they get to this point, they become like cancer. They take the life out of you and your sales career.

Negative Declarations

- "All I get are people who are upside down."

- "I can't get a person who wants to buy to save my life."

- "This place is dead."

- "I can't make any money selling cars."

Whether you are asking yourself the "why" questions or have advanced to the level where you are making negative declarations, you can change now by starting to ask yourself better, more positive questions. This can be as easy as asking yourself questions that begin with the word "what." "What" questions force you to seek better answers.

Positive Focus Questions

- "What can I do to make this deal happen?"

- "What would motivate me to buy now if I was this customer?"

- "What action should I take to generate more business?"

- "What can I do to build more value in my product?"

You may even take it one step further and start making positive declarations. By doing this, you will be giving yourself permission to succeed, much like a power lifter who steps up to a barbell, facing more weight than he has ever lifted before, and repeats to himself over and over, "I can do it; I can lift this weight."

Positive Declarations

- "I will make this deal happen."

- "Every customer I meet wants to buy a car, and I am just the salesperson to make it happen."

- "I know I can create business of my own."

- "I will build more value in my product than this customer has seen anywhere before, and I will get paid accordingly."

These are only a few examples of the positive and negative questions that you have in your mind directing your focus. You may have internal dialogue that includes questions of which you are not even aware.

Make it your goal to become aware of those questions. You can start now. Take a minute to set this book aside and write down on a piece of paper the questions you ask yourself most frequently. After writing down these questions, assess them and determine whether they are positive or negative focus questions. Now, write an alternative and more appropriate question that you should be asking in place of one of the negative questions. If you are having trouble thinking of a question, you may be able to start by writing this one down.

Negative Question

- "Why can't every day be this good?"

Positive Alternative

- "What do I need to do to make every day as good as this one?"

Some of you may be wondering, "Hey, didn't he use that negative sentence at the beginning of this chapter?" The answer of course is yes, and if you didn't think to yourself, "Why would someone ask such a negative question as this after such a great day?" then you may be giving your self-questioning abilities more credit than they deserve. You may be in such a habit of asking yourself these wrong questions that you don't even realize it. If this is the case, then I will ask you again to set this book aside, take out a piece of paper, and write down the questions you ask yourself. To help do this, envision yourself in the situations you have encountered lately, and think of the questions you asked yourself. Write them down on the paper.

If you are still having a hard time remembering the questions you asked yourself, then fold up the piece of paper and keep it in your pocket. Take it out of your pocket whenever you find yourself asking a question that is determining your focus, and write it down. Later, review what you have written, and develop a better alternative to replace it.

The Impact of Words

"It is our attitude toward events, not events themselves, which we can control. Nothing is by its own nature calamitous—even death is terrible only if we fear it.

—Epictetus

Much like the questions that we use as part of our thought process in developing our perceptions are the words we choose when classifying a particular person, place, thing, or situation. The words we use help our minds define and understand the world around us. Each time we select a word to describe something, we are making a decision as to how we want our minds to perceive it. We are labeling it. It becomes part of our internal dialogue.

Each of these labels that we use has the ability to create a totally different emotion or perception inside our minds. These emotions influence our attitudes toward the people, places, things, or situations with which we are contending. Worse yet, when our internal dialogue turns into an outward expression, we begin to influence those around us in a negative fashion.

Stop and think for just a moment about a certain situation you may have faced and how the words you chose to describe it influenced your emotions and your resulting attitude. Maybe it was a time when you had to make a speech in front of a large audience for the first time. Were you petrified or just nervous? Maybe it was a time when someone did something with which you didn't agree. Maybe that someone was a customer, and they made a statement that offended you. Were you outraged or just a bit irked? Sometimes, just by simply choosing the wrong word to label the situation, you will create an emotion that causes you to react in an inappropriate manner. You may have even overreacted because you described the situation to yourself using the wrong words. The words you chose to describe the situation sent the wrong message to your mind. This is also true of the words you choose to label your customers and their circumstances. It is a crucial element in determining the attitude you have toward them and your resulting actions.

The effect that words have on one's attitude became clearer to me when I took a job as a finance manager for a dealership. On an hourly basis, I was approached by one salesperson after another with a credit report and application in hand for my review. Each salesperson, for one reason or another, felt the need to give me their interpretation of the deal as they handed it over. Some would state, "This customer has a few credit issues, but I think there might be something you can do with it." Some of them even elaborated by pointing out positive aspects of their customer's situation by declaring, "They have a big down payment," or, "They have great income and a long time on their job." This, however, was only the case some of the time. Others would begin their assessment with statements such as, "This person has horrendous credit," and then proceed by bringing every negative aspect of the deal to my attention. To the latter salespersons, these customers were a problem and were wasting their time, and so they wanted to get rid of them as quickly as they could. They even used derogatory terms such as "deadbeat" or "credit criminal," and, as much as I hate to admit it, some used terms much worse, such as "roach" or "slug," in an attempt to express their feelings about their customers' present state of affairs.

Over the course of time, I began to realize that the words the salespeople were using to describe their predicaments were not accurate descriptions of the situations they were involved in at all. They were, however, accurate representations of the attitudes they had toward them. In a short period of time, I noticed a pattern emerging. It seemed that in each instance when a deal with horrible or horrendous credit was presented to me, the presenters remained the same. Equally true was the fact that the deals that showed the most promise were consistently presented to me by the former group of salespeople. "Could it be," I wondered, "that some salespeople always get the customers with horrible credit, while others only get customers that have slightly questionable or marginal credit but still show great potential for a deal?" Or was it more realistic to believe that these salespeople were allowing their vocabulary to influence their perceptions and their resulting attitudes toward the situation?

The answer came to me one afternoon in the form of a phone call. It seemed that a customer had decided to take it upon herself to subvert the salesperson and call me directly regarding her financing. After all, the salesperson had not even bothered to call her back since the day she had completed a credit application. Given that she was unable to recall her salesperson's name, and her name did not sound familiar to me, I proceeded to look up her name in the computer to see if we had any record of her on file. The more I looked with unsuccessful results, the more evident it became that one of our salespeople had dropped the ball. Rather than continuing on a hunt for information that I was almost positive was buried deep in someone's desk drawer, I decided to start fresh and gather her information directly. By the time our conversation was complete, I had submitted her application to the bank and found a vehicle that would work perfectly for her wants, needs, and budget. Within a matter of five minutes, she was approved by one of our lenders, and I had set an appointment for her to come see me directly.

The following evening when she arrived for her appointment, I was alerted to her presence in the showroom by the salesperson who had originally waited on her. He poked his head in my door and stated, "Mrs. Jones is in the showroom. I waited on her last week, and she has horrible credit." He continued, "I don't know how she got your name, but she asked for you." I responded by telling the salesperson that I would handle the situation and that he could go back to whatever he was doing. Almost with a sigh of relief he concluded, "Great, I have wasted enough time with her. I need to get a real customer."

I'm sure by this point in the story you have figured out how shocked the salesperson was when Mrs. Jones drove away in her new vehicle. He was shocked because he had grown so accustomed to categorizing any customer with credit issues as having horrible credit that he found it impossible to believe she could actually finance a car. He saw a few credit issues on her report and decided that the word "horrible" would best describe her situation. This label that he applied influenced his focus, which

Is Your mind/ Process connected to Emotion About Customer? WHAT IS IT?

in turn affected his attitude to the point that he did not even attempt to find a solution to the customer's problem.

Consider how the words you use affect your emotional state, and consider the attitude that you derive from it when you are working with a customer. How might you feel about spending time with a customer who has horrendous or horrible credit versus the way you would feel toward someone that just has a few issues or blemishes on their report? Would you act any differently toward either one? Would you focus more on the problem or the possible solutions?

To many of you, it may not seem like a big deal; after all, it is just a word, right? When you refer to your customer using extreme expressions such as the words "horrible" or "horrendous," you are determining how you want your mind to perceive your customer's circumstances. With just one word you are influencing your own mind's perception of the situation. You are telling yourself to perceive the condition as hopeless or as a waste of time. With just one word, you are influencing your focus. You are focusing it on the problem. As we learned earlier, problems are something we look to get rid of any way we can. After all, is a waste of time something you have a positive attitude toward? Probably not—none of us like to waste our time.

Take the time to analyze the words you employ on a daily basis—those you use to describe customers and situations you encounter. Make a list of the negative words you use, and write down a positive alternative for each. When you start doing this, you will notice there are many more negative ways to describe a situation than there are positive, so be sure to guard your vocabulary from new words and catchphrases that are so prevalently thrown around in dealerships today.

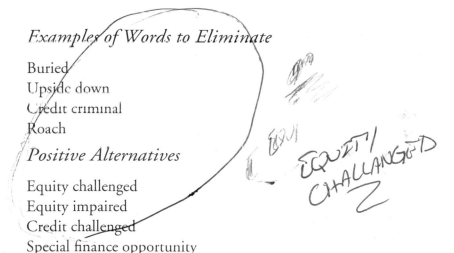

Examples of Words to Eliminate

Buried
Upside down
Credit criminal
Roach

Positive Alternatives

Equity challenged
Equity impaired
Credit challenged
Special finance opportunity

So far we have looked at how our internal dialogue affects our attitude. We have seen how the questions we ask ourselves direct whether we focus on solutions or problems and how the words we use to label the people, places, things, and situations around us affect our perception of them. While having this knowledge of how our internal dialogue works and putting it to use is beneficial to maintaining a positive attitude, we should also become aware of all our external influences and begin to manage them.

"There is little difference in people but that little difference makes a big difference. The little difference is attitude. The big difference is whether it is positive or negative."

—W. Clement Stone

External Influences on Our Attitude

Each and every day, your senses are bombarded with information—some good, some bad. All of this information influences your mental state and affects your attitude. The effect may be very minor, or it may be extreme depending on the content of the information and how directly it relates to your life.

If you were to monitor this information closely, you would probably find that you are being exposed to more negative-influencing information than positive, and believe it or not this is not just true most of the time but as much as 80 percent of the time. That's right. On average, about 80 percent of what you hear and see on the television, in the newspapers, on the Internet, on the radio, or while socializing with others influences your outlook in a negative manner. There just aren't as many feel-good stories out there as there are stories about crime, corruption, and social injustice that seem to spread from one person to the next like a wildfire.

Even in a place like a car dealership that thrives on maintaining a positive atmosphere, you will find that you encounter more negative influences than positive. No, you will not find negative quotations on the wall in the meeting room. No, they do not send out memos about how bad business is at the present time. However, I think anyone that has ever worked in a dealership can attest to the fact that it is easier to find a group of salesmen standing on the front porch discussing how slow business has been and why customers aren't coming through the front door than it is to find a group of them standing around talking about how great their opportunities are in the car business or how fair they find the new pay plan to be.

Over time, consistent exposure to this negative input can take its toll on even the best of us. It beats on us from all directions like the waves beating against a ship in a storm at sea. This continual battering eventually weakens our defenses and destroys our attitudes. This personal destruction is why you must diligently protect the amount of your exposure to negative influences.

Uncontrollable External Influences

Some of the external influences in your life are uncontrollable. If you seek out information about the world around you, interact with other human beings, and live a normal life, you will be exposed to a considerable amount of information that may have a negative influence on you. Furthermore, since you have chosen a career in automotive sales—a career that rewards the performance of those individuals who interact successfully with the buying public—you are guaranteed additional exposure to it.

In a perfect world, all of our customers would arrive at the dealership in their paid-off trade and greet you with a smile at the prospect of going home in a new car. In reality, we know this is not the case. We know that with each new customer we face comes the possibility of meeting someone who has a negative expectation regarding the upcoming event. All too often your customer will direct the apprehension they are feeling in the form of a negative comment aimed in your direction. At the very least, they will have a story to share openly with you regarding a bad experience they have had in the past with a salesperson or service department or with an automobile they have owned. Some may even express their discontent by damning the entire business in which you make a living. This is a hazard that comes with the territory, and you cannot let it affect your performance.

But how, you may ask, do people listen day in and day out to the griping of one customer after another and not let it affect their attitudes about themselves, what they do for a living, or the customers with whom they are dealing? This is where you must realize that your best defense against the effect of continual negative input is a positive offense. Like a professional running back who trains his body all week long for the repeated abuses he takes physically on a Sunday afternoon, you too should train your mind to fortify it against the pounding many customers will try to give your attitude. This is what the superstars of this business and any other profession do to make themselves great and maintain a peak level of performance. They strengthen themselves by training and continuously trying to find ways to improve themselves.

Just as the professional athlete exercises his body and strengthens his muscles, you, too, must exercise and train your mind for the job you perform. You can do this by reading motivational books and articles during the slow times at the dealership, by listening to tapes on your way to and from work, and by attending seminars that may give you a new perspective. You must do these things on a regular, consistent basis to combat the effects that constant exposure to negative influences can have on your attitude. Remember that in the battle against these negative influences, if you are not looking to improve and move forward, then you will be continuously pushed backward and weakened.

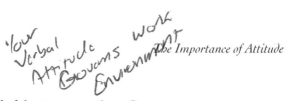

Your Verbal Attitude Governs Work Environment

Controllable External Influences

"Tell me what company you keep and I will tell you what you are."

—Miguel de Cervantes

As I mentioned earlier in this section, a car dealership thrives on its ability to maintain a positive environment. Nonetheless, you will find that there are still avoidable negative influences that seem to thrive in almost any showroom. Some of these influences may be as far away as the front porch, and some may be as close as the desk right next to you. Regardless, these negative influences exist, and you may even consider some of them to be your friends. They happen to be some of your fellow salespeople.

As you know or will soon find out, while working in a car dealership you may have a considerable amount of time when you are not actively working with a potential customer. Rather than using this idle time for productive activities such as making follow-up calls, mailing out thank-you letters, or brushing up on product knowledge, many salespeople will dwindle their days away by socializing with the last people in the world that are interested in buying an automobile from them—other car salesmen.

As the saying goes, "Idle hands are the devil's tools." This is also true of idle minds. When facing this downtime, often your attitude will fall victim to it as you congregate for hours at a time philosophizing tirelessly about everything from the best-tasting coffee in the break room to the fairness of life itself. These conversations may start out innocently enough as harmless chitchat but eventually turn to the topic of the car business.

After all, this is what most car salesmen know best. With this will come their in-depth analysis of everything they think is wrong with the customers, the business, the management, the dealership, the manufacturer, or even the service and parts departments. Some of these salesmen believe they have it all figured out, and they are more than willing to share with you all of the reasons they are unable to sell more than five cars each month and why you shouldn't be able to either. They may have themselves convinced that if the management team, finance manager, or service department were better, they would sell more cars. If the used-car inventory was better or if the customers had better credit, they would sell more cars. In reality, if they just stopped spending all of their time focusing on everything that is negative, they would have a better attitude and more time to do the job they are there to do in the first place: selling vehicles.

When you choose to spend your time with these "I've got it all figured out, but only sell five cars a month" salespeople, you are making a conscious decision to expose yourself to a negative influence. The people you choose to spend your time with when you are not selling cars are a controllable external influence. If you elect to spend it with the underachievers, listening to them gripe and moan, eventually your attitude will be affected by what they are focusing on and verbalizing outwardly. Consider this: would you seek out self-improvement and motivation by sitting in the conference room and watching training videos preaching all the reasons you should not be able to sell a car today? Do not spend your idle time with negative salespeople and then become one of the salespeople who scurry away the moment a customer pulls onto the lot because you are not in the mood to deal with them. Avoid these salespeople like the plague. After all, this is exactly what their negative views are to your attitude and sales career. They are a killer plague, and you want to be at the top of your game the second that next customer rolls up on the lot. Instead, seek out and surround yourself with people who will influence you in a positive manner. Seek out the winners. Surround yourself with them, and they will elevate your level of performance. They will help you stay at the top of your game.

Yes, these winners are harder to find. In many stores, these salespeople make up a very small group. Remember, most elite groups are small, so be careful not to lower your standards for the simple fact that you are alone. As the saying goes, "It's lonely at the top."

Rules for Maintaining a Positive Attitude

1. Change your direction by changing your focus.

2. Change your focus by changing the questions you ask yourself.

3. Stop using words that have a negative impact on your focus.

4. Monitor and control outside influences.

You may be thinking, "My attitude has worked to get me this far, hasn't it?" and you would be correct. Your past is somewhere for you to learn from; it is not where you want to live. You should learn from past experiences, whether good or bad. The possibilities of what you can accomplish with the right attitude are endless. This is why it is important for you to constantly monitor and manage it. It is not something you can pay attention to occasionally. Every single day, life throws curve balls at you, and your attitude will determine whether you stand still and get hit by the ball or whether you smack it out of the park.

Just as attitude is important in your development as a sales professional, so is sincere enthusiasm. Chapter four discusses enthusiasm in detail, demonstrating its effect on the success and longevity of your sales career.

CHAPTER FOUR
ENTHUSIASM SELLS

"Enthusiasm is at the bottom of all progress. With it there is accomplishment. Without it there are only alibis."

—Henry Ford

If I had a dollar for each time I heard an older, more experienced salesperson say, "A new broom sweeps clean," "He's just a flash in the pan," or "It's just beginner's luck," when referring to the so-called "green pea" that had never sold cars before but was managing to turn every "up" he encountered into a commission for himself, I would have retired a rich man many years ago.

After witnessing what I believed to be this true phenomenon, commonly referred to by many as "beginner's luck," repeating itself time and again with each new, enthusiastic salesperson that hit the showroom floor, I began to realize that it wasn't luck at all. Luck was merely the name other people used when they couldn't explain outstanding results derived mostly from simple unbridled enthusiasm in action.

"Experience and enthusiasm are two fine business attributes seldom found in one individual."

—William Feather

This is the type of enthusiasm that causes the "newbie" to spring from bed with anticipation every morning and show up an hour early for work each and every day because nothing is more important to him. This is the same enthusiasm that pushes him out to the curb to take that extra "up" five minutes before closing on a Saturday evening and, in turn, causes him to stay an extra two hours to deliver yet another vehicle. It's the type of enthusiasm that elevates the "green pea" past all of the experienced, highly trained professionals to the top of the sales board during his first month on the floor. This is the type of enthusiasm I am referring to.

"There is no such thing as chance or accident; the words merely signify our ignorance of some real and immediate cause."

—Adam Clarke

If you have trouble believing in the remarkable power of enthusiasm, then stop and think for just a minute. Is it more rational to believe that this new salesperson who has no experience, very little training, and no customer base just happens to have been gifted with the golden horseshoe of car selling or that success is due strictly to luck? Perhaps it is more realistic to believe that their successes are due mostly to the blind trust and unbridled enthusiasm that has helped them overcome obstacles and sell cars in the face of adversity.

"A salesman minus enthusiasm is just a clerk."

—Harry F. Banks

If you have been selling cars for any length of time, sit back and imagine for a moment a time in your past when you had very little experience at the job or task you were starting, but yet you possessed a passion that could not be stopped by any means. Nothing anyone could say would have stopped you. No obstacles could be put in your way. Everything was just a challenge waiting for you to find the solution. You didn't have the knowledge you needed, but you had the zeal to meet anything head-on. This is the effect enthusiasm has on your outlook.

Enthusiasm changes your entire perspective. It converts obstacles into challenges. It transforms the lesser-experienced, knowledge-lacking salesperson into a superstar. You, like many others, may write this off as nothing more than bull and rely strictly on your knowledge, ability to negotiate, and the dealership's ability to supply you with a never-ending supply of "ups." Or you will get smart and come to the realization that enthusiasm is the ultimate secret weapon of all the great salespeople in this business. It is what transforms an average salesperson into the best of the best. Ask yourself, "How much more effective would I be if I were as enthusiastic about my job now as I was the first day I started?" Imagine what adding that level of enthusiasm—combined with your present knowledge and experience—could accomplish. It is a recipe for success.

"You can't sweep other people off their feet if you can't be swept off your own."

—Clarence Day

This unrelenting, consistent enthusiasm is what it takes to be one of the greats in this business. Enthusiasm will allow you to rise to the highest levels you can imagine. Without enthusiasm, you are gambling with every customer you meet that your product, your price, and your dealership are better than your competitors. You are taking the emotion out of the sales process. You are refusing to use your secret weapon. You are forgetting that you are not just selling cars; you are selling people.

Facts, figures, and prices may help you to push a few pieces of metal over the curb, but enthusiasm sells people. If you can sell people, you will sell more cars and make more money. Use your secret weapon; it is what makes you more than just a fact-spouting, key-getting, demo-taking, give-away artist. Enthusiasm is the heart and soul of the salesman.

As the title of this chapter suggests, enthusiasm sells. Enthusiasm sells people. After all, how could a customer who has been going from one boring dealership to another all day not be inspired by someone who is excited to meet him or her and is enthusiastic about doing his or her job? Think of the people you have met in your life. Do you remember every salesperson or clerk that you met, especially the ones that were just going through the motions? Do you remember someone you have met who seemed so overjoyed at your presence that you thought he was going to come out of his skin because he was getting to talk to you? What about the salesperson that was so excited to demonstrate her product that, even after you told her ten times you couldn't buy, she still showed you something about it that excited her? It is a safe bet to say that the enthusiastic salespeople made more of an impression on you, and, in the end, even if you didn't buy from them, you still may have thought, "Wow, they sure were excited. If I ever buy, it will be from them."

"Nothing is so contagious as enthusiasm."

—Edward Bulwer-Lytton

Now on the other hand, if you're employed as an engineer, enthusiasm may not rank as high on your list of important characteristics for professional success. As a salesman, your livelihood depends on your interaction with people. Success depends on the level of enthusiasm you have for what you are doing. Success depends on how strong your conviction is for your product and requires that your enthusiasm is conveyed and used to inspire everyone with whom you come in contact. Your enthusiasm must be contagious. When your customers sense your strong conviction for something and sense your enthusiasm, instinctively they begin to want to be part of whatever it is you are offering, even if it means that they may be going against their own instincts. When you possess this conviction, you become a salesperson. Your enthusiasm and conviction are so strong that they have a powerful effect on your customers, causing them to rethink their positions. It is this element of the sales process that makes customers stop and think, "Do I really need to go look at that other car, or do I really need to do a little more price shopping? After all, I would really love to be a part of what he is offering." Instinctively, people have a deep-rooted desire to be a part of something great. Some of the greatest men in the world have used no more than their conviction for a cause and their outward enthusiasm to inspire millions of people to act on an idea.

Unless you plan to be just a mediocre salesperson, you must master the art of inspiring the people with whom you come in contact. Remember, enthusiasm is contagious. And if you are outwardly enthusiastic in all of your actions with everyone you meet, you will surely inspire many more people to buy your product and to do business with you than someone who is just going through the motions. Why then, as shameful as it is for me to admit, do many of the automotive salespeople I have met in my career only increase a customer's level of enthusiasm when they shake hands, hand out a business card, and say good-bye? Maybe these salespeople are happy being average. Maybe they just don't believe in the power of enthusiasm. Maybe they are just content with earning only a little bit more than if they were working a drive-thru window at a fast-food restaurant. This reality should come as good news to you; your competition is thin when it comes to being the most enthusiastic salesperson a customer has met. No matter what the business, today there does not seem to be much enthusiasm in the workplace. When a customer is met with enthusiasm, it makes the process of buying an unforgettable experience.

"Enthusiasm is that temper of the mind in which the imagination has got the better of the judgment."

—William Walburton

So what exactly, you may ask, is this thing that we refer to as enthusiasm? We have seen the results accomplished by a person consumed with it. We have been told over and over, "Be enthusiastic." In every Saturday-morning sales meeting, your sales manager may tell you that you need to be enthusiastic with every customer. Do we really know what it is and where it comes from?

To begin to understand enthusiasm, it is helpful to understand what the word means. The English word "enthusiasm" was derived from two ancient-Greek words: *en,* meaning "in or within" and *theos,* meaning "god." When combined, they form the word *entheos,* which means "having the god within."

Although today we do not necessarily consider everyone with enthusiasm to be inspired by God, we do recognize that they are being inspired by some great driving force, passion, or desire from within themselves. Your passion may be rooted in your desire to earn an abundant income, or it may come from your sense of accomplishment and desire to be the best. It may just come from the excitement of performing a new and challenging job. Whatever it is, you must make sure you feed it frequently.

"Catch on fire with enthusiasm and people will come from miles to watch you burn."

—John Wesley

If your enthusiasm is the fire within you, then your passion and desire are the fuels that keep it burning. As with any fire, you must continually add fuel to keep it burning strongly; if you do not, it will burn out. Surely everyone reading this book has heard of burnout. Does it occur when you have a lack of knowledge for your product? No. Does it happen when you need a little more training? No. It happens when you lose your enthusiasm. You cannot wait until the fire of enthusiasm has dwindled down to a smoldering pile of ashes or, worse yet, until it has burned out completely. You need to feed it daily, maybe even hourly if necessary. Consider this: is it harder to restart a pile of ashes or to add fuel to an already blazing inferno?

This may sound easy at first, but doing business each and every day with great amounts of enthusiasm is, in reality, far more difficult to accomplish. Whether you are an experienced automotive salesperson with a great attitude or a "green pea" brimming with unbridled enthusiasm, there will come a time when you feel your conviction to be truly enthusiastic about your career choice challenged either by your familiarity with the task at hand or by the repetition and predictability of the entire process.

"One man has enthusiasm for 30 minutes, another for 30 days, but it is the man who has it for 30 years who makes a success of his life."

—Edward B. Butler

Picture yourself at your dealership on a Saturday. It is three o'clock in the afternoon, and everyone at your dealership has already sold a car; some have even sold two. You, on the other hand, started your day with the rudest person you could have imagined, and furthermore he consumed three hours of your time only for you to discover he owed ten thousand dollars more on his car than it was worth. After enduring his insulting jibes and the declaration that salesmen are all crooks, you find enough motivation inside yourself to try again, and you wait on another customer. This next scenario plays out slightly differently, however. This couple is nice to you and, with the exception that they wanted to take a fifteen-minute test-drive in four different vehicles before making a decision, you find them very easy to deal with. They are even willing to commit to buying your car today if you can get them financed. After all, they need a car badly because the bank just took theirs back yesterday. To top it all off, it is the last day of the month, and you need to sell just one more car to hit the bonus you were relying on to make your overdue car payment.

This, to me, does not sound like the start to a day that would help fuel my enthusiasm for selling cars. It may even be enough to make some of you doubt the reason you are even in this business. If the latter is true for you, then you definitely need to establish a plan for maintaining your enthusiasm and monitoring it regularly.

Some of you may find that by simply managing your attitude, you will automatically maintain a healthy level of enthusiasm. Some others may find that even with a positive attitude you still feel something is lacking. You have an empty feeling about the work you are doing or the accomplishments you are achieving. You need more to motivate you. You need to get the excitement back that you had the first time you started selling cars. You need a change.

"The worst bankruptcy in the world is the person who has lost his enthusiasm."

—H. W. Arnold

This may be why so many salesmen move from one dealership to another. It may not really be in search of better floor traffic, better inventory, or a better pay plan. It may be the feeling of a need for change to help them find a little of the enthusiasm they once had. For some people, a new store can do this. Be cautioned: it doesn't last long. Off to the next dealership they go, believing yet again that the grass is greener on the other side. In reality, they fail to recognize the true problem lies within themselves.

If most of the salespeople who jump from one store to the next would stop and examine the situation, they may find that by monitoring themselves and the conditions that affect their enthusiasm a little more closely, they can make the changes that will have a lasting effect and establish a lucrative career at the dealership where they presently work.

"Nothing great was ever achieved without enthusiasm."

—Ralph Waldo Emerson

You can be responsible for your level of enthusiasm. First, take a look at the things in your life that sap your enthusiasm. Identify and evaluate them.

Things that Sap Your Enthusiasm

- **Stress**

Stress is an unpleasant state of emotional and physiological arousal experienced by people in situations that they perceive to be dangerous or threatening to their well-being. It is real. It is normal. It happens to everyone. Stress is often described as an event or situation that causes tension, pressure, or negative emotions. It is a process involving a person's interpretation and response to a threatening event.

Each time you feel stressed, your body responds physically. According to Webmd.com each time your body is stressed your blood pressure rises, your pulse quickens, your blood-sugar levels rise, and your digestion stops. Your memory may even begin to fail. This all sounds quite threatening. However, in moderation, stress seems to improve motivation and performance on less complex tasks. It can help to prepare you for the situations you encounter on a daily basis. It helps you become more prepared to focus on the task at hand, to generate new ideas or ways to accomplish things, and to meet deadlines or quotas. At these acute levels, stress gives us the extra edge that we need.

Without it, we would have very little energy or motivation. Stress is healthy—at the right level. Stress also motivates us to achieve and fuels creativity.

If, however, these levels of stress persist on a continual and prolonged basis, then the physical changes occurring in your body increase to levels that are no longer beneficial to you. This chronic stress has the opposite effect on your performance. It causes adverse reactions in your body such as fatigue, eating disorders, hypertension, sleep deprivation, and depression, to mention only a few. None of these things can be associated with maintaining a high level of enthusiasm. Stress can even be the cause of your demise. Everyone needs to assure the cycle of stress and recovery. Recovery allows you to handle stress the next time. This recovery may be referred to as "coping." Coping means using thoughts and actions to deal with stressful situations whereby we lower our stress levels. There is much to be learned about stress. Learn about it, and help yourself in your career and in your life in general.

- **Boredom**

Boredom is the feeling of being tired and impatient. You may be tired of and slightly annoyed by a person or situation that is not interesting, exciting, or entertaining. The cause of boredom may be the routine of doing the same job for a long period of time that creates an atmosphere for you which is no longer challenging. This lack of a challenging environment may make you begin to question yourself and your job. Questions like the ones below begin to make you doubt your own self-worth and hamper your enthusiasm.

Is this what I am going to spend the best years of my life doing?

Is this all I am destined to become?

Look at your reasons for being bored. Consider what you can do to make your job more interesting and rewarding. Often we must take the actions to cure our boredom. Don't expect others to do it for you. You are the captain of your ship and the master of your fate, so to speak.

- **Failure**

What is failure? To put it simply, it's the lack of success. At one time or another, we will all experience failure of some type. For some of us, these failures can be major setbacks, while for others they may just be disappointments or letdowns. The cure may be that we need to make a few minor adjustments in the way we do things. But no matter who you are, if you repeatedly face one failure after another, your enthusiasm will begin to diminish. This is one of the hardest aspects for new salespeople to deal with. They see each customer they have talked to and didn't sell as a failure.

- **Attitude**

In case you haven't figured it out after reading chapter three, your attitude affects everything. Without a good attitude, there is no possibility of being enthusiastic when dealing with your customers. Even if you can fake a good attitude outwardly when you are with customers, your overall career will suffer if you lack the right attitude to maintain your enthusiasm.

- **Abuse**

The verb "abuse" means to hurt or injure by maltreatment. All abuse is not of the physical nature. It may be emotional. With customers yelling at you and sales managers barking orders in your direction, it is easy to see how a salesperson could begin to feel abused. This abuse by others may be the thing that you find will take away your enthusiasm the fastest. This abuse will attack more than one aspect of your enthusiasm. It can result in feelings of failure, which increase your level of stress and in turn affect your attitude. As we have discussed previously, all three of these things will rob you of your enthusiasm. After all, who would be enthusiastic about going to a job where the boss told you how much of a loser you are for not selling a customer. A who spent the past two hours of your time telling you how you were a crook because you were, as he put it, "crazy" and trying to gouge him on the price of your car and a thief for what you offered him on his.

After reading everything I have written about the situations that can have an adverse affect on your enthusiasm, you may be thinking, "Wow, what a bummer. I thought this book was going to help me sell more cars, not bum me out." (If you think reading it bummed you out, you should imagine trying to be the writer!)

There is good news! Now that we are aware of the situations that may be holding us back from being enthusiastic about our jobs, we can begin to modify some of our own perspectives and behaviors. We may not always be able to control our environment, but we can make changes in ourselves that lessen the impact it has.

Combat the Situations that Sap Your Enthusiasm

- **Take a step back and put things into perspective.**

"If it is not something that is going to affect your life a year from now, it probably is not something that is important enough to worry over in the first place."

This single phrase changed the way I prioritize the amount of worry or stress that I am willing to devote to any single situation. The dealer who said this to me probably did not realize that he would not only realign my perspective about the situation I was dealing with at that time, but he would also realign the way I evaluate all potentially stressful situations from that point on.

I began to realize that I was expending much more energy on problems in my life than they required. Whether they were personal or business issues, I was wasting valuable time and energy on things over which I had no control, and it was sapping my enthusiasm.

I witness salesmen every day worrying themselves to the point that they can't even wait on a customer over issues that are not even important enough to be given a second thought in the first place.

One salesperson I worked with would worry himself to the point of frustration over the fact that another salesman had sold a vehicle and made a good commission. He thought he deserved it and couldn't understand why it wasn't his deal even though he had nothing to do with it. His level of stress over what he felt was an unfair situation affected him to the point that he would spend the rest of his day on the phone with his wife, complaining about it, and would forego the opportunity to wait on customers coming into the store. Of course, every salesperson would like to have just sold that "good deal" that just rolled over the curb. However, it makes no sense to let it cost you the next opportunity. Don't get stressed out about things over which you have no control.

Now you might not be as bad as that salesperson, but do you let situations stress you out unnecessarily? Do you get upset when you find out that you have to split a deal because someone logged it on the phone log? Do you lose half a day stressing out when the accounting office makes a mistake on your check that you can't get corrected until Monday? If any of this sounds true, then you need to reassess your priorities. Business has these small setbacks, but you will end up losing in the end if you devote a disproportionate amount of time worrying about them. This business is stressful enough without adding to it ourselves.

Whenever you find yourself in the middle of a stressful situation that is sapping your enthusiasm, just ask yourself one of these two questions.

Question One

"Is this something that is going to affect me a year or more from now?"

If the answer is no, then put it out of your mind until a more appropriate time, not when you should be making a living selling cars.

Question Two

WOULD A COMMISSION HELP THE PROBLEM?

"Is this a problem that would be improved if I was out there on the showroom earning a thousand dollar commission?"

If your answer to this question is yes, then you need to go make it happen.

These two questions alone will help you put more of your problems and stressful situations into perspective. Once you begin assigning the stressful issues in your daily life their appropriate level of thought, you will begin to be more enthusiastic about your day.

- **Continue to learn.**

You may wonder why learning helps your level of enthusiasm. The answer is actually very simple. When you learn new things and continually seek new information, you are improving yourself, which helps to increase your level of self-worth. New information also stimulates new ideas, which inspire you. This inspiration is just what you are looking for to fuel your enthusiasm. Add your improved self-worth to your new knowledge, and you will be enthusiastically seeking an opportunity to demonstrate the new knowledge you have gained. In addition, you have arrived at where you are today by continually learning new things. If you look back at your life, you will find that each time you made a concerted effort to learn something new, the knowledge not only enriched your life, but it also helped make you just that much better at what you were doing or got you closer to what you wanted to become.

If you think learning new things does not help your level of enthusiasm, just examine the alternative. Once you stop learning new things, you begin to become stagnant. Worse yet is the fact that once you stop improving on the foundation of knowledge you already have, you don't just stay at that same level, but you go even further backward. You begin to regress, forgetting things that you once learned. This is not much different than if you exercised and lifted weights for years and stopped. Not only would your muscles stop growing, but they would begin to shrink to the condition they were in before you started exercising. I don't know about you, but the thought that I am not much better or smarter than I was yesterday or last week—or for that matter even last year—because I thought I already knew enough doesn't do much for my enthusiasm for my life or my work.

This practice of continuing to learn as a form of motivation does not have to be limited to information about the car business or selling. You may find that just by expanding your knowledge in other areas of interest you will feed your enthusiasm for life.

I found this to be true every time I became interested in learning something new or when I found a new hobby that required me to learn something different. I would become more enthusiastic about life in general, and it would automatically carry over into my business life. It gave me a greater purpose in life.

Try it! The next time you notice that you are lacking enthusiasm, reach out for that extra bit of knowledge. It may just be what you need to give your enthusiasm a boost. You may find something that amazes you enough that it excites you to the point where you look forward to the next opportunity you will get to share it with someone. That someone may be a customer, and he may just be amazed enough at how enthusiastic you are that he buys from you instead of from someone else.

"Enthusiasm is the inspiration of everything great. Without it no man is to be feared, and with it none despised."

—Christian Nevell Bovee

- **Have a goal. See the bigger picture.**

If you knew that one day you would be as successful as your wildest dream, how enthusiastic would you be about life? If you knew that someday you would own your own car dealership, that you would make more money than you could ever spend, that you'd live in the biggest house in the neighborhood, and that you'd drive the nicest car in town, then you would meet each day with a smile knowing that you are getting one step closer to realizing that dream. Would you be bored? Probably not, because you would be too busy pursuing your destiny. Would you worry about every failure you encountered? Doubtful. You would learn from them and view them as just steps in the process that is getting you closer to your ultimate goal. Would you feel stuck in a rut? Of course not, because you would know that you have a bright future ahead. You'd meet each day with enthusiasm, knowing that everything is part of a bigger plan.

Consider the alternative. What if you have no goals? With no goals, you have no foundation upon which to base your inspiration. What if you have a dream, but you don't work toward it? What if your big picture, your big dream, is only to be able to pay your bills this month? That might keep you motivated enough to sell the numbers of cars necessary to earn a check big enough for you to scrape by in life, but would you be enthusiastic about it? Sure, you might be motivated—motivated by the fact that the bills are due—but I seriously doubt that you would be enthusiastic.

Inspire yourself by setting a goal and working toward it a little each day. Dare to dream, and seize every day as an opportunity to do something that will bring you one step closer to that dream. You are in the car business, a business with unlimited potential. You determine how much you will make and how successful you will be. Make that determination, and pursue it every second of the day. Be in control of your life.

"Enthusiasm is the yeast that makes your hopes shine to the stars. Enthusiasm is the sparkle in your eyes, the swing in your gait; the grip of your hand, the irresistible surge of will and energy to execute your ideas."

—Henry Ford

CHAPTER FIVE

ESTABLISHING RAPPORT

From the deals that are negotiated between scores of attorneys in boardrooms for some of the largest corporations in the world to the smallest agreements that are struck between two individuals over the smallest things, the success or failure of any business is determined by the relationships that people establish and maintain on a regular and ongoing basis. This too is true of all the business that is being conducted in every car dealership across America. As a salesperson, you are the link between your dealership and the buying public, and your ability to establish and maintain relationships is a fundamental skill that you must master to ensure the dealership's and your own success.

Each time you answer a sales call, strike up a conversation with someone in the service department, or step out to the curb to greet a new customer you are building a bridge between the buying public and the dealership that you work for. You are beginning a relationship—a relationship, in the beginning, comprised of nothing more than two strangers meeting for the first time. This is where it all begins, just two people—complete strangers—with no common ground. It's not the easiest place to start for either one of you.

The depth of these relationships that you establish and foster will greatly depend on your ability to identify with the people with whom you are interacting. By identifying with them, you are establishing a common ground, a rapport, or a mutual understanding. As the word relationship implies, you are relating to one another. Without this common ground, you will merely remain as two individuals, one of whom wants to sell a car and the other who is looking for a salesperson. With no common ground between you and your customer, you will find that the pathways of communications will be limited. Without

Is it Better
to fit them clean
2. Build Rapport
or Push Through
Grabbing keys

Establishing Rapport   83

open and honest communication, it becomes difficult to find solutions to issues that arise throughout the entire sales process.

You are the one looking to sell the car, and it is your job to help open these lines of communication and then cultivate, nurture, grow, and see this relationship through until it blossoms. You must be proactive in finding that common ground, establishing rapport, opening the lines of communication, and relating to your customers and their lives. As a very good friend of mine from many years ago used to say, "You've got to get in their bubble."

Sometimes this is harder than it sounds at first. After all, we live in a world where most of us have been told by our parents from a very young age not to talk to strangers, and as adults we are constantly bombarded with warnings to guard information about ourselves diligently. Terms such as "identity theft," "privacy act," and "fraud victim" have become commonplace in today's society. Who hasn't seen a news story about an elderly person being taken for their life's savings by someone with whom they had a close association? Combine that with the fact that many customers have had an experience or, at the least, have heard stories from others regarding a less-than-savory experience with a salesperson or a car dealership, and you will begin to understand why people are guarded when they meet you for the first time. Very few of them will arrive at your dealership enthusiastically looking to meet you.

With this social climate prevailing in our society, how, you might ask, do we manage to get close enough to our customers to establish any type of relationship with them? First, it is helpful for you to understand what it is that makes your customers tick, what motivates them. To do this you need to get inside their "bubbles." Their bubbles are the small worlds that they have revolving around them. Your customer's bubble includes her passion for her family, her dedication to her work, her extra-curricular activities, and the significance she finds in each of those things making up the world that revolves around her. It is all of the things that are important to her and that, in return, give her a sense of purpose and importance.

This deep-rooted desire to feel important is one of the main things that separates human beings from every other species in the world. Simply existing and living for the sake of living is not satisfying enough. People want to be recognized and acknowl-edged for their importance in the world. They crave justifica-tion for their existence, and they want their due recognition. After all, of what value is it if you have succeeded at the most complex undertakings but you don't get the recognition for it? You feel as if nothing you do is important to anybody. Every-body wants to be made to feel important.

This brings me to my next point. What someone is or what they have accomplished alone gives them no source of pride unless the people around them acknowledge it. It is the people around you that give you that feeling of importance. This is the open door you are looking for. It is within your power to make anyone feel important any time you want. All you need to do is express a genuine interest in them and their lives. By doing so, you will be giving them what they crave and desire. You will be giving them the feeling of importance. Additionally, people like the person who conveys the feeling of importance. They remember them, and this, for you as a salesperson, is a good thing. Once someone likes you, it is easy to establish a relation-ship, and this is your goal.

"Every man is my superior in some way, in that I learn from him."

—Ralph Waldo Emerson

I am not suggesting by any means that you use flattery. Flattery is the complimenting of a person, often excessively or insincerely, especially when it is to gain an advantage according to MerriamWebster.com. In itself, it is insincere and, when detected, can be insulting to the person on the receiving end of it. What I am suggesting is that you become a student of the people around you. Find something that interests you about every person you meet, and learn from it.

If this is not something you are accustomed to doing, you may find it difficult at first. Many salespeople feel it is their job to sell the customer on how great they themselves are. If this is something you are in the habit of doing, you must realize that when you are selling a car it is your customer's time to shine. It is their time to feel important. After all, that is what brought many of them to your store in the first place. They wanted to make a change to one of the biggest status symbols in their life, their automobile. That's right, automobiles are not just a means of transportation anymore. They are one of the top two possessions a person has that exemplifies his or her level of success or importance to the people around him or her.

"When you talk you repeat what you already know; when you listen, you often learn something."

Critical

—Jared Sparks

One salesperson I worked with knew the importance of making people feel important and establishing common ground and, as a result, was phenomenal at getting people to like and want to buy from her. From the moment she met each customer, she acted as if he or she was the most important person in the world, and she wanted to know everything about him or her. She found great pleasure in meeting new people and was enthusiastic about making new friends. Within the first ten minutes, she knew not only her customers' names but also where they worked, what they did at their places of work, how long they had been there, what their children's names were, where they went to school, what grades they were in, and even what their favorite classes were. She would discover what made them important and, additionally, would learn from them. She took a genuine interest in them, and they loved her for it. As a result, she sold more cars than anyone I had ever witnessed and made more money in the process.

I recall a time when two older men—brothers, to be exact—stopped by to browse the inventory during a big sale we were having. The two farmers had just finished reading the morning paper and eating breakfast at their favorite diner when they had decided that—since winter was approaching and they had nothing more to do on the farm—they would stop by to walk off their breakfast and kick a few tires.

Neither one of these men had even the slightest intention of buying a car when they walked in the door. Actually, after looking around, they didn't even see a car they liked. They were there to kill time and walk off breakfast, as the matching toothpicks protruding from their lips helped to confirm. Margie was their salesperson, and how she finally got them to pick out a car

I will never know. However, I soon found out *why* they bought it. One of the gentleman commented to me, "I don't even need a car, but I just can't disappoint Margie."

It was at this point that I realized how powerful the relationships you establish are to the entire sales process. After all, I had never had a customer buy a car from me, especially one they didn't even want, simply because they didn't want to disappoint me. But up until the point when I witnessed that man buy a car from Margie, I never realized how powerful feeding a person's desire for importance was, and she was the master at it. She knew it was the quickest way to get people to like her and want to do business with her.

Each person you meet will be proud of a different aspect of his or her life. These things will be as varied as the individuals themselves. What one person finds to be rewarding, another may get absolutely no satisfaction from. A successful business owner may be proud of the work she has devoted her life to and the accomplishments she has achieved. A preacher may take exceptional pride in his church or the size of his congregation. A grandfather may be proud of his beautiful grandchildren and find enjoyment talking about them for hours.

Some customers you meet will openly advertise the things they are proud of. Some may wear a shirt or hat or pin to tell the world about themselves. Some may have bumper stickers on their vehicles exclaiming, "Ask me about my grandchildren," or, "I love Yorkshire Terriers." Others may not publicize their lives as openly, but all you need to do is scratch the surface with a few questions, and the real individual will come pouring out.

I'll share with you an example I won't soon forget that occurred while I was working in the finance department at a dealership. I was beginning the paperwork with an older couple who didn't seem at first to be very exciting people. As I always do, I struck up a conversation with them by asking where they were originally from (a common question to ask when you live in Florida, due to the fact that the majority of people are transplants from somewhere else). The wife answered by telling me that they were both from Poland.

At that point, the husband reached into his pocket and pulled out a copy of a picture that was folded in fourths and laid it on the desk in front of me. As he pointed to a young Polish soldier kneeling in front of Pope John Paul II, he remarked that it was a picture of himself with the Pope. He proceeded to tell me how he and his fellow soldiers had taken a Catholic cathedral back from the Germans in World War II, and many years later the Pope wanted to meet and thank him for the deed. I could see he was glowing with pride in every bit of the story he told, so much so that he didn't want me to interrupt him with an explanation of any of the paperwork that he was signing. I almost felt guilty each time I had to interrupt his story to disclose the terms of the loan. As far as they were concerned, it was their time to shine, and that was more important than anything I could tell them about the paperwork.

Weeks later when their customer survey arrived at the dealership, I saw that they had commented at the bottom of the survey how great I was to deal with and how I had made them feel like the most important people in the world.

Did I praise them and tell them how great they were? Did I try to flatter them? No. All I did was express a genuine interest in them. All I did was listen.

"The art of conversation is listening."

—Malcolm Forbes

This is what you must do with each of your customers. Make them feel like the most important people in the world. Find out what makes them great and take interest in it. Ask questions. They will like you for this; they will open up to you, and then you can begin to build lasting relationships with them.

Start Building Early

Timing is everything. This stands true when it comes to building rapport and establishing relationships with your customers. If you wait until the negotiation process has begun to start establishing rapport, then you may find that the customer will meet your interest with skepticism. The customer will realize your lack of interest in him or her as an individual, and any attempts you make at this point will seem feigned. To the customer, you may seem like the friend that calls to ask, "How are you doing?" only when she needs something, and we all know how difficult it is to like that type of friend.

The proper time to establish rapport with your customer and express a sincere interest is during all the phases leading up to negotiations, not during them. Additionally, it is always easier to discuss sensitive matters, especially in instances where there is a high likelihood of disagreement, if you have an established relationship to fall back on. It is essential that you have laid the groundwork upfront. Don't wait. Don't let the negotiation process be the first instance when you and your customer try to agree on something. After all, it is easier to agree with someone

Rapport as Negotiating tool

when you have already identified with each other on points of less importance than the ones that will be negotiated. It is even easier if you have accomplished the task of making your customers feel important. They know this feeling is not something they will find at every dealership. This alone strengthens their level of commitment to you and affords you a bit of negotiating leverage. In the end, if they can buy the same product somewhere else, the only thing they are really buying is you.

Important in all of this rapport building is the fact that each person you meet is different. It is important that you identify these differences and interact with each person appropriately, recognizing that he or she comes to you with his or her own set of emotions and varying responses. Some of these responses will be discussed in forthcoming chapters.

CHAPTER SIX

CONTENDING WITH THE FEAR FACTOR

"If there is any great secret of success in life, it lies in the ability to put yourself in the other person's place and to see things from his point of view—as well as your own."

—Henry Ford

How soon it is that many of us forget our first day selling cars—a day filled with excitement, enthusiasm, and anticipation, all a bit tempered by fear of the unknown. We are dealing with thoughts racing through our minds as we approach our first customer. *Will I remember what I learned about selling cars? Will the things the training taught me to do really be effective with a customer? What if I make a mistake?*

Little did we realize at that moment that the consumer we were approaching was dealing with some of the same issues. *What if I buy the wrong car? What if they try to pressure me? What if I pay too much? What if I make a mistake?*

This fear of making a mistake is the number one motivating factor behind the majority of your customers' actions and statements. Different customers may project the emotion of fear outwardly in varying forms. Some may stick their hands out, wave you off, and announce as you approach, "I just want to look around without being bothered." Many more will proclaim, "I'm just looking," or, "I'm not buying today," as you attempt to greet them. Some may even try not to acknowledge your existence as they turn away from you and trudge off into the inventory without so much as a glance. No matter how inappropriate we deem their actions, they are all signs that your customer is experiencing the emotion of fear.

You may protest this concept and cite as an example the increased number of customers that are arriving at your dealership armed with facts, figures, and instructions for the proper approach to buying a car.

It is true that they may be more informed, more assertive, and more prepared to do business. Nonetheless, in order to begin to understand your customers, you must recognize that it is the emotion of fear that has motivated them to make prepara-

tions for this event in advance—in much the same manner you should have prepared when you began your career selling cars.

The emotion of fear, in itself, is nothing more than the emotional part of your brain sending a warning signal to itself and to the rest of your body to prepare for an upcoming event. This is exactly what the customer has done. Does this preparation your customer has undertaken eliminate the emotion of fear or merely demonstrate the extent that some of your customers are willing to go in order to deal with the situation at hand?

If you have ever taken the time to read what is published in books or posted on the Internet about our industry and the process of buying a car, you would realize these advanced preparations may actually have the opposite effect of the one that was initially sought.

The practice of scaring the automotive buying public into believing that without the purchase of a certain how-to book or the help of a particular online buying service it is surely doomed to exploitation by auto dealers has become big business for many companies these days. By saying this I am not implying that there aren't examples of misconduct in the automobile business just as in every other profession. Nor am I saying that a customer should remain ignorant and submit to the pitfalls of making an uninformed buying decision. But these companies, despite all their proclaimed best intentions, make a profit off of their ability to impart fear into the American consumer, allowing this negative image of the automotive-purchasing experience to thrive in the minds of consumers. This in turn helps to intensify the negative emotions that your customers are experiencing and gives them cause for concern regarding their level of preparedness.

Imagine for a moment that you are facing a fearful situation. The situation is one that has an outcome with lasting effects. For instance, say you are going to need a major medical procedure. There is a strong likelihood that you will be fearful of the upcoming event and its outcome. Would an advanced knowledge of all the intricacies involved in the procedure make your fear disappear? Maybe, but that may depend on the possibilities of less-than-favorable complications arising in such a procedure. What if the information you review to prepare yourself consists of many perilous warnings and horror stories about other people's past experiences in the same situation? This would hardly serve to alleviate your level of fear. The same can be said about our customers when they enter our dealerships.

"The man who can put himself in the place of other men, who can understand the workings of their minds, need never worry about what the future has in store for him."

—Owen D. Young

It is due to this fear that a professional salesperson must learn to contend with customers' concerns on an emotional level as well as from an analytical perspective. People like others who try to understand them rather than attack them with facts without regard for their predicaments no matter how true or rational the reasoning may be. They are even likely to feel angry or mistrust the person who immediately tries to persuade them without giving appropriate acknowledgment to their points of view. This may be the reason why, when all things are the same in a given opportunity, a customer will favor the salesperson and dealership demonstrating empathy toward his or her circumstances over the one demonstrating a lack of emotional connection.

Many people may contend that an automotive salesperson can't express empathy toward their customer's situation and still participate in the process of handling objections. This would only be true if a salesperson was trying to pressure someone into buying something he or she has no need or desire to own. Consumers at a car dealership have come to you with a need or a desire and may have unresolved conflicting issues that require addressing. When they object, they are merely expressing to you an internal conflict that they are having about the buying process and are presenting it to you for your help.

An empathetic salesperson has the ability to put himself on the customer's side of the desk in order to facilitate the mutual understanding of his or her particular situation. This allows the salesperson to discover what factors may be inhibiting the sale and, furthermore, enables a rational analysis with the consumer, perhaps presenting an additional perspective on the matter.

In an attempt to do this, many inexperienced salespeople find themselves becoming sympathetic to the customer's plight and feeling exactly as the customer does on the matter. This is how many salespeople become ineffective. They confuse empathy with sympathy, despite the fact that the two are quite dissimilar. Remember, empathy is the understanding of feelings, while sympathy is the sharing of those feelings. It is the understanding of the customer's feelings that is desirable; the sharing of those feelings may prevent you from being effective in a sales situation.

Additionally, empathy is the ability to view the world from that person's perspective without passing judgment or validating the legitimacy of his or her plight. One of the biggest misconceptions about empathy is that you have to be in agreement with someone to feel or express your understanding. Sympathy, on the other hand, is when you actually experience the same feelings as another person regarding a matter. Your thinking then becomes clouded with the same emotions the customer is experiencing.

Clearly understanding the definition of empathy, possessing the ability to feel it, and knowing the importance of what it can do to alleviate the consumer's fear is not enough. You must learn how to express this empathy to the concerned party for it to truly have any impact on the situation. This can be accomplished by utilizing the following three easy steps.

Effectively Displaying Empathy

1. **Listen:** Give your full and undivided attention with the intent of understanding the customer's concerns.

2. **Confirmation:** Ask questions to clarify important points when necessary. This is vitally important, because in failing to clarify the point they are trying to express, the resulting declaration of understanding may seem feigned. An easy way to avoid misunderstanding what you have heard can be accomplished by following these three steps.

    a. **Summarizing**

        - So you mean that…

    b. **Rephrasing**

        - So in other words…

    c. **Questioning**

- Could you clarify that for me?

3. **Convey:** Preempt your dialogue with one of the following statements to impart your understanding to the customer.

- **I can understand that.**
- **I can appreciate that.**
- **I know what you mean.**
- **I can see why you feel that way.**
- **I see what you mean.**
- **I understand how frustrating this must be.**

Using these steps will help you create a productive environment of open communication and mutual understanding in overcoming fearful situations for you and your customer. In addition, you can apply these same steps to diffuse other emotionally charged situations such as contending with angry customers and handling objections, as you will see in upcoming chapters.

EMPATHY IS KING to Rapport

CHAPTER SEVEN

OVERCOMING AND ELIMINATING OBJECTIONS

"If you find a path with no obstacles, it probably doesn't lead anywhere."

—Frank A. Clark

Wouldn't it be wonderful to find the fantasy sales job that didn't require you to deal with a constant bombardment of annoying and occasionally sales-ending objections? Imagine for a moment that everyone wanted the merchandise you were selling, and nobody objected to buying it. All you'd have to do is drive your truck down the road and ring a bell alerting your customers to your arrival, and they would come running, waving fists full of cash. This fantasy job exists, and you are probably more than qualified for it. This, however, may be a job selling ice cream, and you may find it to be a little less than rewarding. You may also find that it doesn't pay quite as well as you'd hoped. You see, the level of difficulty in your job is mostly determined by the problems and objections you encounter on a daily basis, and your ability to handle these objections is what makes you more valuable than an ice-cream vendor.

"Salesmanship starts when the customer says no."

George O. Boule Jr.

"I need to think about it." "I want to sleep on it." "I need to do a little more research." If you have been in the car selling business for more than one day, you have already heard one or more of these three statements from customers, maybe even all three of them from the same person.

The reason I refer to them as statements and not objections is because, in reality, they are not truly objections. An objection is a statement presented in earnest opposition. These examples are merely statements of avoidance based on a hidden objection used to delay the purchase of your product at that particular time. For the sake of ease, we will simply refer to these vague statements customers use to stall as "avoidances." Many times your customers will use these avoidances to camouflage a true underlying concern that, in reality, is their real objection to purchasing your product. Maybe they don't understand something, they are not sold on the benefits of the product, or they are not happy with the pricing.

In the course of dealing with customers, you must keep in mind that many people don't openly express their dissatisfaction with situations. It is more socially acceptable to make an excuse rather than express a negative fact. In fact, many people try to elude confrontation to such an extent that they will even resort to lying to avoid it. Studies have shown that the most common reason given for why people lie is the need to avoid confrontation. To help demonstrate how prevalent the occurrence of lying is to avoid uncomfortable situations, we could examine something as common as a trip to a local restaurant. While dining out, it is not an uncommon occurrence for people, when asked by a waitress how their meal is, to willingly respond that everything is OK when, in fact, their meal is less than satisfactory. They want to avoid confrontation. They will, however, express their displeasure to the restaurant in a more subtle form at a later date by never returning or by merely not tipping as well as they would have had they been pleased with the experience. Our customers relate to us in much the same way. When our customers don't buy from us or when they claim that they'll be back at a later time yet never return, they are simply voicing their objections to us in a more subtle form. Unfortunately for us, our inability to recognize such situations can cost us many sales.

To be a successful salesperson, you must first learn to differentiate between avoidances and objections and the messages being conveyed by both. It becomes much easier to handle them once you can identify them and understand the difference.

Definitions

Avoidances are statements that rarely define the hidden objection of the customer. They are merely used to avoid the uncomfortable situation of dealing with the true objection to purchasing.

Objections are specific statements of concern that a customer expresses to convey feelings for a need to delay the purchase of a vehicle.

Examples

Avoidances

- I need to think about it.
- I want to sleep on it.
- I need to do more research.
- I want to shop around.

Objections

- I can't afford it.
- The payments are too high.
- The price is too high.
- I want more for my trade.
- I can't live with that color.

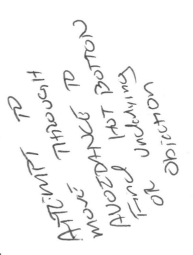

Even though there are many more actual objections to purchasing a vehicle than there are avoidances, you will discover that you encounter avoidances more frequently than objections. Your customer will employ avoidance at any point when progressing to the next level of commitment or when he or she has an unresolved issue. This intensified feeling of commitment or unresolved issue creates a heightened level of anxiety that the customer feels the need to alleviate. By using avoidances to object to the process, he or she is merely trying to lower this anxiety level and impart to you an objection that needs to be addressed. You actually need to see past the avoidance and help raise the objection to the surface.

You may be thinking, "This sounds foolish. Why would I try to create the customer's objection for them?" The reality of the situation is that you are not creating the objection; you are simply helping to identify one that already exists. When you examine the situations you encounter, you will find that more sales are lost when avoidances are overlooked and an underlying objection never surfaces than when a clear objection is exposed and resolved. If you've been selling cars for any amount of time, consider some of your past experiences. Have you lost more sales to people who "just want to think about it" or to customers who express a true objection? Isn't it easier to resolve an objection pertaining to something specific, such as monthly payments or down payment, than it is to persuade people that they shouldn't "think about it" or "sleep on it?"

This is why many customers may feel pressured when they go to a car dealership. They encounter an inexperienced salesperson or manager who keeps trying to persuade them to buy their vehicle when they haven't even taken the time to find out the true underlying objection, let alone address it. A customer feeling pressured is a perfectly normal emotional response to a sales-person trying to persuade him into doing something that his mind is telling him to object to for one reason or another.

Unmasking Avoidances

The process of unmasking avoidances to reveal the true objections can be accomplished in a few simple investigative steps.

Process

- **Pause:** Do not seem overly anxious to address the statement. Remember one of the key reasons people express avoidances is to relieve the stress they are feeling. By snapping back instantly, you are not allowing them to vent that anxiety. You may in fact be increasing it.

- **Empathize:** Acknowledge and express your understanding of their statement. It is easier for them to relate to someone who understands their situation.

- **Simplify:** Help to identify their possible objection.

- **Understand:** Listen to the objection they reveal.

Example

Customer: I want to think about it.

Pause

Salesperson: I can understand your desire to think it over.

Salesperson: In the past, when people have expressed to me the same concerns you are having, we found that it was typically due to one of three things: the dealership, the vehicle, or the money.

1. Do you like the dealership?

2. Do you like the vehicle itself?

3. Is money the issue?

In most cases, one of these three issues will elicit some type of response. If not, you may want to expand on other possibilities.

4. Is it the down payment?

5. Is it the monthly payment?

6. Is it the trade-in amount?

7. Is it the price?

Will asking this list of questions raise every objection out of the customer? No. Nothing in the sales business works every time. I do think, however, that you will be surprised at the number of customers who will voice a true underlying objection as you go through the list. Some will even raise an objection that is not on the list. Customers know you are searching for their true objection, and they will blurt it out like a winning answer on a game show. "It's the color!" some may exclaim and then elaborate, "I just can't live with that color. But I do like that white one over there."

You may find more times than not that a customer's objection will relate to a money issue. These objections can be the easiest to overcome, if you don't jump past all of the other questions before getting to the price issue. Many salespeople jump right to the issue of price. They skip over every other possibility by assuming that this customer has the same issue with the price

[handwritten margin note: walk through questions to help to order]

as previous customers. By doing this, you will find that now you not only have a deal with no profit but also have an objection to contend with.

Take your time. Go over each question one at a time. Often when customers are asked question number four regarding their down payment, they will respond, "Yes, it's the down payment; I won't have it all for another three days." Believe it or not, this is a good thing. It's merely a small problem that you can solve for them—a problem they may not have shared with the salesmen at the dealerships they visited before yours. The other salesmen may not have taken the time to express a concern for the customers and their issues.

You will find that you may get many different answers as a result of using this method, and very rarely will you get to the end of the list and fail to unearth the true objection. This is what you intend to do. By starting with the most unrealistic problem, the dealership, and working your way through all of the points of the deal, you ensure the customer is comfortable with every aspect of the deal, with the exception of the concern he or she has brought to your attention. Now you just need to overcome it or eliminate it entirely.

Handling Objections

"In theory it is easy to convince an ignorant person; in actual life; men not only object to offer themselves to be convinced, but hate the man who has convinced them."

—Epictetus

Many salespeople in or out of the car business have difficulty dealing with customers' objections. Some salespeople may even try to avoid them all together. This is a perfectly natural response to a word that typically carries such a negative connotation. When people object to something, it is typically believed that they oppose it altogether. We may even believe that people are so moved by their convictions that they are willing to argue the point on which their objection is based. This is not necessarily the case when encountered in sales.

The professional salesperson needs to view the objections encountered as nothing more than expressions of concerns that customers convey when they are considering buying from him or her. Objections are a positive sign and are not only welcomed by good salespeople but also anticipated. Objections are a positive sign that a customer would like to buy from you if only he or she could resolve an issue. Treat objections as questions, not as points of argument.

When confronted with an objection, you can use one of two solutions to resolve it. You can either overcome the objection or eliminate it entirely. Since customers have an average of five objections during the sales process, it can often be more beneficial to eliminate objections than to try to overcome them. We will look at both of these options.

 ## OPTION 1—*Overcoming Objections*

When you attempt to overcome an objection, you are simply trying to persuade the other party to see things from a new point of view and agree with it. You are tryin[g]
customer. You are trying to get the customer t[o]
you are saying. You are trying to change his or h[er]
by presenting additional information.

Customers do not always lend themselves easily to being converted to another's line of thinking. You are asking them to change. Think of how difficult it is for you to change, even when you have wanted to. Think of the biggest change in your life. Did it occur after a rational analysis of a situation or after an emotional experience?

Buying is an emotional experience for many customers, so it only seems natural to base your reasoning on emotion rather than on a strict analysis of facts. This is where the "Feel, Felt, Found" approach proves to be useful.

Process

- **Pause**: Do not seem too anxious to counter their objection with a reply. This pause not only allows the customers to digest what they have just said but also affords them time to make additions to it, which may be to your benefit.

- **Understand**: Be sure to show empathy by demonstrating that you clearly understand their objection and express that to them in your response.

- **Compare**: Relate their situation to one that you have seen yourself or that others have faced and share what they discovered when they looked more closely.

- **Summarize**: Conclude that it is the "right thing" for them to do, and encourage them to buy.

Example

Customer: I can't afford payments of three hundred dollars a month. I am only paying two hundred and fifty now.

Pause

Salesperson: I understand how you feel about making a payment of that amount. Other customers that I have dealt with in the past felt the exact same way as you at first. Then they found that by owning a new car with a warranty they would be saving enough on repairs to more than justify the additional fifty dollars a month that they were spending for the new car.

Consider the following for a moment: if you spend two hundred dollars on a set of new tires, two hundred for a new alternator, and two hundred for a starter, then you are spending six hundred dollars a year for repairs on top of the payment you are making now. That averages out to about fifty dollars more a month just to drive your old car. Add the amount you are paying the mechanic to the amount you are paying the bank, and you find that you are already making a monthly payment of three hundred dollars. You just don't have the new car to show for it. Are you ready to start driving that new car you've been paying for all along?

Rule to Remember

- It helps to mentally convert objections into questions in your own mind. This allows you to get some insight into the dilemma your customer may be facing.

Example objection: I can't afford payments of three hundred dollars a month.

After converting it to a question: How could I myself rationalize making a payment of three hundred dollars a month if I was in their position? (Objection Conversion)

OPTION 2—*Eliminating the Objections*

Despite the fact that the "Feel, Felt, Found" method of overcoming objections has been widely used and successful for many professionals in the automotive business for many years, some customers have evolved to a point where they are becoming less emotionally involved in the buying experience and require that the dealership make concessions to eliminate their objections. If used properly, the process of isolating objections and then eliminating them to appease the customer can also benefit the sales process.

- **Pause**: Do not seem too anxious to counter the objection with a reply. This pause not only allows customers to digest what they have just said but also affords them time to make additions that may be to your benefit.

- **Understand**: Be sure you clearly understand their objection.

- **Eliminate**: Isolate the issue and the objection, and hypothetically eliminate them. You can eliminate more than one objection at a time by using the isolation method.

- **Re-propose:** Propose a plausible solution to the objection.

Example

Customer: The payments are too high.

Salesperson: If I understand you correctly, you are telling me that the payments are the factor stopping you from proceeding, is that correct?

Customer: Yes, they are too high.

Salesperson: Hypothetically speaking, if the payments weren't too expensive, is there anything else that would stop you from buying the car today?

Customer: No, I guess not.

Salesperson: Then let's work at making these payments more affordable for you.

Rule to Remember

- If you must eliminate, isolate.

By using this method, you have the opportunity to eliminate the process of overcoming multiple objections since you isolate their main concern and resolve it. You will find that many people are willing to overlook their less important objections if they feel that you are making concessions to accommodate the one concern that is most important to them. If you fail to isolate it, however, then you may find that the customer will create a new objection each time you eliminate the last one.

The Importance of Pausing

"Some will never learn anything because they understand everything too soon."

—Thomas Blount

I am sure you have noticed in each of the examples I used above that I was sure to note the need to pause before addressing your customer's objection. Frequently salespeople are too quick to react to an objection expressed by a buyer. They may not even allow the customer to finish his or her statement before they interrupt with, "But..." This is considered a reaction to a customer's concern. Reacting to an objection only magnifies the anxiety that the customer was attempting to dispel. You must pause so that you can gain your composure and respond rather than react. Responses are controlled, and reactions are not. Remember to respond, not react.

Be attuned to the fact that many customers simply think aloud. They may be coming to terms with the situation at hand and inadvertently expressing their thoughts aloud. They occasionally overcome their own objections.

Example

Customer: I can't afford payments of three hundred a month.

Salesperson: (Pauses before responding.)

Customer: Well, I guess with what I have been spending for repairs in addition to the payment I have been making, I have been spending an average of three hundred dollars a month anyway. A car payment of two-fifty a month plus six hundred a year in maintenance averages three hundred dollars a month.

A customer overcoming his or her own objections is not a common occurrence. However, if you don't allow the opportunity for this by pausing, you decrease the chances of it happening to zero.

Timing Is Everything

Many salespeople are guilty of trying to overcome objections too early in the sales process. Try to remember that there is a time for everything, including addressing customers' objections.

A good example of this is when salespeople try to overcome a price objection while still in the greeting, presentation, or demonstration phase of the selling process. The salesperson hears a price objection and automatically tries to overcome it.

Trying to overcome or eliminate objections too early in the sales process can actually be counterproductive. When you try to overcome an objection prematurely, customers will detect your resistance to their concern, and you will be compounding the stress of an already stressful situation. Smart salespeople utilize premature objections to lower the level of stress for the customer. With a lower stress level, customers become more cooperative. Let's look at how this is accomplished.

Example

Objection occurs during presentation or demonstration drive.

Customer: Well, I think the price is too high.

Salesperson: I can understand exactly how you feel, and I wouldn't expect you to buy it unless the price was suitable for you and your budget.

Since this is not the time when you should be negotiating the price, you lower the customer's stress level by showing empathy toward him and his situation. You have not eliminated or even overcome the objection and will have to address it again at the appropriate time, but you have conveyed to the customer that your level of expectation is no higher than his at this point. Remember, people object when they begin to feel an increased level of commitment to you or your product.

So when is the right time to overcome or eliminate objections? As a general rule of thumb, you shouldn't try to overcome any objection that doesn't pertain to the vehicle, its options, or the presence of all concerned decision makers until you are inside the dealership at the desk asking for a commitment or presenting numbers.

Anticipating Objections

Automotive-sales professionals encounter objections every day. One in particular is so common and difficult to overcome that some salespeople have come to accept it as a valid reason why a consumer can't purchase a car at that time. This objection occurs when a person is considering buying a vehicle and brings up the fact that they must consult with their significant other. What car salesman hasn't heard "I need to talk to my wife" from a customer who has test-driven, discussed numbers, and possibly even committed to buying if the figures are agreeable? Why don't we anticipate it? Maybe we are afraid of creating an objection. The truth of the matter is, if you are dealing with a person who is shopping without his or her spouse, you have a much better chance of hearing this objection than you do of it not coming up at all. It is an objection so commonly wielded that the few people who will buy without consulting their spouses may utilize it as avoidance even if it is not their real objection. This is referred to as a higher-authority objection.

The most effective way of dealing with this objection is to eliminate it early in the process by addressing it as soon as possible. Ask, "Do you think your wife would like this car?" By the response, you will know whether or not this is going to be an issue that you will have to contend with later in the sales process. When I say you will know by the response, I mean that if they say anything other than, "She doesn't care what I buy," or its equivalent, then you need to include that significant other in the process early on. Suggest that the other decision maker be picked up while on the test-drive.

You may think of the number of males you see entering your dealership and think, "Why does he keep saying wife?" Do women have that much influence over their husbands' buying decisions? Just look at these facts from RoadandTrack.com and eWomenNetwork.com and you will see why.

- Women make 80 percent of all retail purchases.

- Women influence 80 percent of all household buying decisions.

- Women sign more than 80 percent of all checks.

- Women purchase 65 percent of all new cars.

- Women influence 85 percent of all automot
  decisions.

Based on these facts, it is easy to see why the spouse (higher authority) objection should be anticipated and addressed early in the sales process. In the event that you proceed without including the spouse, you will find yourself negotiating the deal twice—once without and once with the significant other—or you will find yourself with no deal at all.

Professionals Deal with Objections All the Time

The process of dealing with objections not only creates a dilemma for customers but also is a struggle for many salespeople. As professionals, we do not want to give the impression of being "high pressure" or too aggressive. As a result, many salespeople fail to address objections or avoidances. The end result in this situation can typically be characterized as a lose-lose situation. The customer who came to your dealership looking for all the right reasons to buy from you and your store left without accomplishing his or her goal. You spent time selling the features and benefits of your product and the positive points of conducting business with you and your dealership, and in the end you didn't make a deal.

This is where a salesperson needs to be aware of the difference between being assertive and being aggressive. As professionals, it is our job to be assertive. Our job is to share with our customers the positive aspects of our merchandise and its benefits, as well as to help clarify any information that may aide our customers in making an informed decision.

Many of the most honorable professions work in much the same way. Imagine for just a minute that you are a doctor, and you discover that a patient has the beginning stages of an illness. When you inform her of her status and recommend a treatment, her fear compels her to shrug it off and say, "I'll think about it and get back to you." At that point, would you simply get up from your desk, thank her for coming, and hand her your card? Of course not. You would continue to counsel her and possibly address some of her concerns. This is what professionals do.

Remember that contending with objections is a natural part of the sales and negotiation processes. It is unavoidable. If you find that you are not contending with many objections, it is probably because you aren't asking for your customers' commitment to buy a car from you. Frequently in the sales process, objections will arise when you attempt to gain this commitment. In the following chapter, we will look at the importance of obtaining and keeping this commitment.

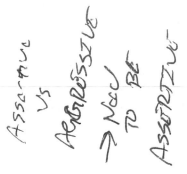

CHAPTER EIGHT

THE COMMITMENT

If the entire process of overcoming objections, negotiating the price, and closing the sale were the parts of an animal, then the spine that would hold it all together would be the commitment. Realizing that the commitment is the backbone to effectively negotiating and closing a car deal is paramount to becoming adept at negotiating and closing car deals successfully.

The commitment in itself is an acknowledgment by the customers to themselves and, more importantly, to you that they have found a vehicle they like and desire to purchase from you right now; not later today, tomorrow, or next week—they will buy it now.

Anything less than acknowledgment to buy right now means you do not have a committed customer. Gaining this commitment is the first step toward negotiating and closing your deal. This may sound simple enough; however, it is a concept that must be remembered first and foremost with each and every deal you are involved in, or you will find yourself participating in a one-sided negotiation process. One-sided negotiation involves you giving prices, followed by discounts, and then concluding with the customer leaving the dealership without purchasing.

"OK. Thank you for all of the information. I'll think about it and get back to you." If you have ever heard these words after giving a potential client all of the information they needed to make an informed decision, including an outstanding deal, and still didn't sell the car, then you should have learned how crucial getting a commitment from your customer is to the entire sales process.

In the remainder of this chapter, we will examine the best time to ask for the commitment. We'll explore the most effective ways to get your customer committed and the effect the commitment has on the rest of the sales process. More impor-

tantly, we will look at ways to keep the commitment once you have it.

When to Ask for the Commitment

When is the right time to ask your customer for a commitment? The best and only right answer I can think of is, "After you <u>have</u> earned the right to ask for it." Only after you have taken the time to establish rapport with your customer, to select a vehicle based on their wants and needs, and to give them a top-notch product presentation and demonstration drive have you earned the right to ask for a commitment.

Gaining the Customer's Commitment

The first step toward securing a commitment from your customers comes after you have done all of the previously mentioned steps. After your return from the test-drive, you will first want to make sure to confirm your customers' satisfaction with the vehicle they have driven. You can accomplish this easily by asking a question directed at them and their level of satisfaction with the vehicle and the vehicle alone. This is not the time to try and close your customers or get them committed to buy from you today. This is when you make sure the vehicle will not be the issue that concerns them and gauge their willingness to purchase from you. Some questions you may want to use to ensure they are satisfied with their vehicle selection are as follows.

"Excluding the financial aspect of the transaction, is this a vehicle that you would be happy to own?"

*"Putting all financial considerations aside, is this a
would be happy to own?"*

"If money had nothing to do with the transaction, would this be a car you would be happy to own?"

By asking these questions, you will get one of two responses. You will either obtain a statement of their satisfaction with the vehicle selected or an expression of their displeasure with certain aspects of it. This will either allow you to move on to the part of the process when negotiations begin or give you more information on finding a vehicle more suitable to them. Either way, you will be headed in a direction that ultimately can lead to selling and delivering an automobile.

Once you have determined you have chosen the right automobile, you can then proceed to the negotiating table. This is the first real opportunity to ask your customers for their commitment to buy the car. This is best done before you begin discussing numbers, before you begin negotiating payments or price. This is designed to bring out the objections your customers may have before the financial aspects complicate the process. The only apprehension many of your customers will express at this point is their concern with the monetary portion of the deal.

If you are able to raise, isolate, and then eliminate any objections beside those concerning the monetary aspects of the transaction before negotiations begin, you simplify the negotiation process. You simplify it by narrowing it down to nothing more than both parties agreeing on acceptable figures. After all, if you have raised and addressed all of their concerns up front, then the only issue to address will be the financial aspect of the deal. You will find that the sooner you contend with an objection presented at the negotiating table the better.

Every salesperson may have a different way they feel comfortable asking a customer to buy from them, but essentially the same question needs to be posed to each customer no matter what words you choose. The following questions are designed to bring the objections out of your customer.

"Can we schedule delivery of your new vehicle now?"

> Fundamental ?

"Are you prepared to buy this car and take it home today?"

With questions such as these, your customers will be sure to raise any concern that they may have. However, you will probably find that more often than not your customers will have already begun expressing their concerns throughout the beginning stages of the sales process. This being the case, you may want to revert to an anticipatory question when seeking a commitment. An anticipatory question includes the concern that your customers have expressed previously, combined with a request to do business if their demands are satisfied.

Go BACK TO PREVIOUS CONCERN TO

"If the price/payment is right, are you prepared to drive your new car home today?"   WRAP QUESTION

"If I can get you enough for your trade, are you ready to take this new car home today?"

"If I can get you in this car without a lot of money down, are you ready to take this car home today?"

"I know that you mentioned earlier that you didn't want car until after the holidays. However, if I could make it so t

payments didn't begin until well into next year, would you buy today?"

By asking these questions, you will get one of three things: a conditional commitment, an avoidance, or an objection. In chapter seven, we learned how to contend with objections and avoidances. Below are examples of contending with these factors while trying to obtain a commitment using some of the techniques you have learned.

Conditional Commitment

- "Yes, if the payments are right."

- "Yes, if the price is right."

- "Yes, if you get me enough from my trade."

Straightforward Objection

- "The price is too high."

- "I don't think it is in our price range."

- "I don't have any money to put down."

Avoidances

- "Well, we really need to think about it first."

- "Like we told you before, we aren't buying today; we are just looking."

- "Well, we are not quite sure this is the car we want. We haven't looked around enough."

All of these responses are good. Some are better than others, but all are still good responses to receive from a potential client. After all, none of them expresses the customer's complete opposition to buying a vehicle from you. If the customer gives you one of the first three conditional commitments, then it is advisable to clarify his or her intentions by repeating it back to them.

Conditional Commitment

Customer: Yes, if the payments are right.

Salesperson: Great, then I will let the manager know that you are ready to do business today if the payments are right. Is that correct?

Customer: Yes.

Repeating your customers' words back to them may seem a bit repetitive. However, once negotiations begin, many customers conveniently forget they committed to buy from you earlier. By using the practice of repeating their words back to them, you acknowledge your understanding of their intentions, thus helping to firm up the level of their commitment. It lets them know that you not only heard them tell you they were going to buy, but you also understood the commitment and expect them to honor it.

Straightforward Objection

Dealing with straightforward objections can be accomplished using the same anticipatory questions as above.

Customer: The price is too high.

Salesperson: I can fully understand your concern with the price. Most of my customers have the same concerns as you. Except for the price, is there anything else stopping you from buying this vehicle and taking it home today?

Customer: No, just the price.

Salesperson: Great, then I will tell my manager that you are prepared to take this vehicle home now if the price is right. Is that correct?"

[handwritten: → I only ask to see if there is something I can do]

Customer: Yes.

[handwritten: → tie down]

Avoidances

You will find more often than not that many customers will not express their true concerns as openly as the customer who gives you a conditional agreement or a straightforward objection. They will have objections or may even mask their objections behind avoidances. Why then do so many salespeople stop asking for a commitment when avoidances are used? It may be fear or lack of training, or maybe it has just become politically incorrect to ask people to do business with you after you have done your job and earned the right to ask for their business.

If your customers respond to your request for a commitment by using one of the common avoidances or something similar, their answers may be motivated by the emotion of fear. After all, they probably have many unanswered questions in their head. How much will I need to come up with for a down payment? What are my monthly payments? How much can I really buy the car for? What will my interest rate be? How long will I finance it? All of these questions generate fear in the customer's mind. It is the fear of making a mistake.

As we discussed in chapter six and as described by wcbmd.com, fear is nothing more than the emotional part of your brain sending a signal to itself and to the rest of the body, warning it to be prepared for an upcoming event. That is exactly what the customer's brain is doing. The customer may feel she will be better prepared if she shops more, thinks more, reads more, or, in the reality of things, just postpones the situation. You may find that by acknowledging her current position (showing empathy) regarding the vehicle and most importantly the price, your customer may feel more at ease with the situation.

Example

Customer: Well, we really need to think about it first.

Salesperson: I can understand your desire to think about it. Many of my customers have felt the same way as you do now until they found how affordable I could make the vehicle for them. Just so I can clarify the situation, is it the vehicle itself you are thinking about, or is it the payments that are your main concern?

WHERE IS FEAR?

Customer: (Gives objection) Like we told you before, we aren't buying today, we are just looking.

Salesperson: (Responds) I can understand that you feel the need to look around, and many of my best customers felt the same way. After further investigation, we normally found that it was really one of three things stopping them from proceeding with the transaction. These three things were either the dealership, the vehicle itself, or the monetary aspect of the transaction.

Then ask the customer:

1. Do you like the dealership? Does it seem like the type of place you would feel comfortable doing business?

2. You said earlier that the vehicle is one that you would be happy to own. Is there some aspect of the vehicle you are unsure about?

3. Is money the issue?

By asking these questions, you increase your chances of drawing out the customer's true objection to purchasing now. Not assuming that every customer is truly in a position to buy. However these are the questions that if you fail to ask will ultimately result in your all too frequent disappointment. Your disappointment at the truthfulness of mankind when you call the customer back the following day only to be met with a brief explanation that they bought elsewhere after they left your store. Did they find a better vehicle? Did they get a better price? Maybe they just met someone who wasn't afraid to ask the difficult questions.

Get It with an Offer

In the event that a customer does not give you a commitment before the negotiation process, do not let this stop your progression to the next step. Do not be the reason they don't buy. Proceed to the next step. Show them some numbers. Many times you will find that avoidances will turn into objections when they see the numbers. The scenario may play out something like this.

Guys w/
Low Ball
PRICING,
RE-FRAME
THE QUESTION
"WHAT IS
The monthly
PRICE You
ARE LOOKING
F.OR?"
THEN
Bull
Commitment

The Commitment   129

You present the numbers to the customer. Almost as if by natural reflex, she reacts by saying, "Well, that payment is way too high," or, "Oh no. I would want a lot more for my trade."

At this point, you simply convert her objection into an offer with a commitment to buy at her figures.

Example

Salesperson: Just how close to this payment/price did you have in mind?

Customer: Well, I wouldn't pay any more than three hundred dollars per month.

Salesperson: So, if I understand you correctly, you would buy this vehicle today if I can get it for you for three hundred a month. Is that correct?

Customer: We really just came in here to look. But if you could get our payments down to three hundred dollars a month on that vehicle, we would buy it now.

Salesperson: Great. I will let my sales manager know what we need to do to earn your business today.

(? BALLSY)

If your customers do react to the numbers with one of the common reflex responses previously mentioned, I have found that it is helpful to try and entice them. By trying to entice them, you are provoking them to give you a committed offer that they would be willing to buy it today.

This technique turns the larceny in every car buyer's heart against him. Nobody can resist a great deal. Many times, at the

Handwritten margin note (left, vertical): # WHAT ARE THE PARAMETERS That would cause you to make The Purchase.

prospect of saving a large amount of money, a customer will forget any of their previously mentioned objections and proceed to engage in the process of negotiations. This is the same customer who, after signing the buyer's order, looks at you and says, "We really didn't plan on buying a car today."

Example

Customer: No, those figures are too high, but we are just looking today anyway. We are not ready to buy now.

Salesperson: I can understand you are just looking, but my own curiosity has me wondering. Is there any figure that would be so enticing that you would be unable to pass it up today?

Customer: Well, there is a figure, but I seriously doubt you would accept it.

Salesperson: Don't worry. You won't insult me. Tell me what figure would entice you enough to buy this vehicle today?

Customer: Well, I would buy it now if you sold it to me for twelve thousand dollars.

Salesperson: Great. I will tell my manager that you will buy the car if the figures are agreeable to you.

At this point, you may not have a deal. However, you do have a committed offer. This is at least a starting point for the negotiation process. Now you just need to agree on the numbers.

Handwritten note (bottom): Doesn't MATTER The offer Only The Fact That We are coming to The table

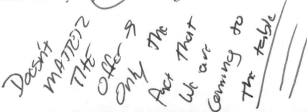

Keeping Your Buyer Committed

If getting the commitment were the most important aspect of the negotiating and closing processes, then keeping the customer committed would have to be a close second. What purpose would it serve to get a customer's commitment only to lose it a few minutes later? Every salesperson has felt the frustration of getting a customer committed only to have him "back up" or have second thoughts when he realizes he is close to buying a car. Here are three simple rules to help you keep the commitment once you have it.

1. Repeat the customers' words back to them.

By repeating the customers' words back to them, as we demonstrated in a previous example, you are helping to cement the customers' words to their actions. This eliminates the possibility of any confusion between you and the customers' intentions.

2. Define the commitment in writing.

We have all heard the expressions, "It's right there in black and white," and, "Seeing is believing." These two sayings, which most of us have heard since we were children, have a very strong influence on the reasons that we get a customer to sign a committed offer. After situations such as the examples above, it is advisable that you put it in writing. Remember, most misunderstandings arise from a lack of understanding, so put everything in writing. Additionally, if someone is willing to put his or her signature on a committed offer, then he or she is truly committed. Conversely, if someone is not willing to sign, then he or she may just intend to back up on a verbal commitment after obtaining more information on your position.

"A verbal contract isn't worth the paper it is written on."

—Samuel Goldwyn

Example

Write the following statement on the sales worksheet for the customer to sign.

Mr. Jones agrees to buy the vehicle now for $12,000.

X_____

3. Get cash down.

Cash down—or "glue," as it is effectively referred to in many car dealerships—is the strongest type of commitment you can secure. A common phrase that accurately defines the importance of getting cash down (or a check, as the case may be) is, "Put your money where your mouth is." Once customers are willing to put up the money to back their offer, they are truly committed.

Some salespeople become bashful when it comes time to ask for a good-faith deposit. They may even feel it is an unnecessary step. However, you are selling a big-ticket item and engaging in a process of offers and counteroffers. Just as in real estate (another big-ticket item), a good-faith deposit is an expected token to solidify a prospective buyer's commitment to an offer.

Don't be bashful; start at the top. Ask for all of the money.

Example

Customer: No, those figures are too high, but we are just looking today anyway. We are not ready to buy now.

Salesperson: I can understand you are just looking, but my own curiosity has me wondering if there is any figure that would be so enticing you would be unable to pass it up today.

Love THAT LINE

Customer: Well, there is a figure, but I seriously doubt you would accept it.

Salesperson: Don't worry. You won't insult me. Tell me what figure would entice you enough to buy this vehicle today.

Customer: Well, I would buy it now if you sold it to me for twelve thousand dollars.

Salesperson: Great. I will tell my manager that you will buy the car if the figures are agreeable to you. Write me a check for twelve thousand dollars.

Sure, this may at first sound a little excessive. However, over the years I have heard responses ranging from "I will need to finance it" (this information can be helpful since most customers who are financing are truly payment buyers) to "I don't have a check. I brought cash." Regardless of whether you receive all of the money as a good-faith deposit with the offer, by asking for it all you are demonstrating to the customer just how serious you are taking their offer.

The initial committed offer you receive from a customer may not be an acceptable offer on the vehicle they wish to purchase. However, you still have a commitment to buy. Now it is just a matter of negotiating the terms of the sale. In the following two chapters, we will look at some helpful principles regarding the process of negotiations.

YOU ONLY WANT Commitment TO MOVE FORWARD

→ You come IN, KNOWING THE PRICE. IS THERE AN ISSUE WITH THE CAR or with the Budget?

CHAPTER NINE

NEGOTIATIONS:
THE PARTIES INVOLVED

"Let us never negotiate out of fear, but let us never fear to negotiate."

—John F. Kennedy

The act of conducting negotiations in its simplest form has been defined by *Riverside Webster's II Dictionary* as "to meet and discuss with another in order to reach an agreement." At first this may sound like a simple task. However, when examined more closely, as it pertains to the automobile industry, it is a much more complicated process than this simple definition would have you believe. In the next two chapters, we will examine the parties involved in the process of negotiating a car deal and some commonly held principles and methods for negotiating. First, let's look at the most basic elements of the negotiation process: the parties involved and the roles they assume.

The Salesperson as a Negotiator

The first element we will focus on is the ingredient of the entire process we should learn to gain the most control over—ourselves. Each of us is the one aspect that remains a constant factor in each of our negotiations. Since it is foolish to think that we can fully control all of our customers, the best way we can improve our position at the negotiating table is by strengthening our own negotiating skills and by diversifying and preparing to adapt to a multitude of situations.

Some salespeople seem to exhibit such a natural aptitude for the negotiation process that others may have us believe that negotiating is a natural-born talent. To the contrary, this could not be further from the truth. The ability to negotiate successfully is a learned skill. Some people's lives and previous experiences have resulted in the development of their negotiating skills to the point that the process appears to be second nature to them. Their environments and other outside influences have groomed them for activities such as negotiating, just as yours may have prepared you for other elements of the sales process. Similarly, you may have grown up in an environment that affords you a vast amount of technical or product knowledge, or maybe you had an early fascination with the mechanical aspects of automobiles. This may be an area in which others find themselves lacking. Whether you need to begin learning about negotiations from scratch or you have years of experience, there is always more to learn or improve upon. A good negotiator starts to become less effective the minute he believes that he knows everything there is to know about the subject.

Practice Makes Perfect

"Experience is something I always think I have until I get more of it."

—Burton Hills

Understanding the information in the following three chapters regarding the negotiation process is only the first step you must take on your journey to becoming a skilled negotiator. The knowledge you gain and the techniques you learn must be practiced, refined, and possibly even redefined until they become habitual. The better you become at applying the information given to you in these chapters, the stronger your position will become at the bargaining table.

Imagine for a minute that you want to learn to play golf or even improve upon an already good game. You may seek out a book to read or a video to watch on the sport, or you may even enlist the instruction of a club pro to coach you on the finer points of the game. Learning from these sources alone will give you a better understanding of the techniques useful to improving your game. However, the real progression will not begin until you implement and practice what you have learned on a regular basis so it becomes second nature to you. The same can be said regarding the knowledge you gain apply on your path to improving your negotiation skills.

Some may assume then that the only way to gain experience with the negotiation process is to get involved in real-life situations. Regardless of the fact that the experience you gain from being "under fire" is undoubtedly an invaluable source to learn from, there are still other ways to improve your skills without putting as much at risk. An effective and very convenient way to familiarize yourself with the process without directly getting involved is by observing and evaluating other salespeople while they are engaged in negotiations with their customers. By watching and listening to others absorbed in the process, you are able to critique and evaluate a real-life situation from an objective point of view. Through this, you will see how the customer and salesperson interact with each other, how the conversation that transpires, and more importantly, the outcome of each session. In time you may find you discover just as much, if not more, from other salespeople's successes and mistakes as you do from your own.

While observing others may serve to acquaint you with the process of negotiations and will even provide you with valuable tools to draw from in the future, you still must become proficient at applying the knowledge you have gained during your actual interactions with your customers. This can best be accomplished by role-playing with people around you.

Many salespeople spend time educating themselves about the vehicles they are selling long before they ever shake a customer's hand, or they arm themselves with information regarding the rebates and incentives available from the manufacturer before they ever test-drive a client in a vehicle. However, they fail to make advanced preparations for the negotiation process. By taking the time to sit face-to-face with someone and role-play, you will begin to gain knowledge of your own strengths and weaknesses. It is only once you begin to understand your weaknesses and limitations that you can determine where you need to make improvements. I'm sure you'll agree that it is a lot less expensive to learn from a mistake while you are practicing than it is to lose a sale because you weren't prepared. Staying with the scenario of improving your golf game, this would be the equivalent of practicing your swing on the driving range instead of waiting until you enter a tournament where the winner could receive a substantial payout.

Furthermore, just as you might practice different swings from various distances, you will also want to vary the type of people with whom you role-play. While enlisting the help of your friends and family members may help you to become proficient, you may want to practice with people with whom you are not as familiar. After all, you want to become proficient at negotiating with people you cannot easily predict. This can be accomplished by incorporating sessions into your routine that require the assistance of your fellow coworkers.

Finally, you must make sure that you learn the most you can from every real-world negotiating situation you experience. Take the time to assess your performance after you finish interacting with customers whether you were successful in selling them or not. This evaluation should encompass both the positive points of your interaction and the negative ones. It is just as important to learn from what you did correctly as it is to acknowledge what you could have done better. Many salespeople miss valuable opportunities to gain knowledge about themselves and the negotiation process by focusing more on what they can spend their commission on rather than on what they did to get it in the first place. Conversely, when a sale is not completed, a lot can be learned—even from a negative experience.

Fundamental Principles of Negotiating

Over the years, I have witnessed countless instances when the salespeople negotiating a deal became their own biggest roadblock to the sale. Sure, you will have many instances when customers do not buy cars because of factors that are beyond your control (payments or price are too high, customer owes too much on trade, etc.). However, to be a successful negotiator, the first thing you must ensure is that you and your actions are not the reason your customer doesn't complete the sale. Believe it or not, there are many salespeople who allow the one thing they should have the most control over to sabotage their deals. To help avoid this, you should know there are some fundamental principles that a diplomat must always remember when trying to foster a productive negotiating environment.

Fundamental Principles

- **Never let it get personal.**
- **Don't get impatient.**
- **Don't argue or disagree.**
- **Control your ego.**

Never Let It Get Personal

Many salespeople and customers alike find it difficult to maintain an objective point of view during the negotiation process. An objective point of view is one that is not influenced by emotion or personal opinion. This may sound like an easy task at first, but when examined closely it is found that keeping an objective view can be the biggest hurdle encountered by many salespeople. With both sides presumably having so much at stake, negotiations can at times become heated. When one side feels they are on the losing end of the process, they may instinctively react by feeling personally threatened or even insulted. As a professional salesperson, you must remember that even when the customer is getting the best of you, it is to your advantage to keep things in perspective and remember it isn't personal, so don't let it get that way.

"Men are not against you; they're merely for themselves."

—Gene Fowler

Don't Get Impatient

Impatience can be your worst enemy when trying to conduct successful negotiations. Always try to be mindful of the fact that this is a big decision for the customer, who is in an uncomfortable environment. Your impatient behavior may be just the thing that pushes the customer out the door. Even if your feelings of impatience are not noticeable to your customer, they are still not conducive to a favorable negotiating environment. These feelings will ultimately lead you to feelings of frustration and will affect your ability to think rationally. If you begin to think irrationally while in the negotiation process, you will soon discover that you are fighting off the urge to become angry with your customer. Once you are experiencing true feelings of anger, you are no longer competent to perform your job correctly. Although this is not the only way anger enters into the negotiation process, it is definitely one of the main ways. In this sense, you will find that patience truly is a virtue and is rewarded accordingly.

"A man is about as big as the things that make him angry."

—Winston Churchill

Don't Argue or Disagree

"Arguing with a fool proves there are two."

—Doris M. Smith

There is bound to come a time when a customer says something with which you don't agree—maybe even something that you are confident is absolutely incorrect—and your first reaction will be to jump at the chance to prove your knowledge and correct him. Quite frequently, I witness salespeople disagreeing with customers and arguing their points until the customers concede to the salespeople's thinking and then proceed to leave the showroom corrected but without a new vehicle. A salesperson that has disagreed with a customer and possibly even taken it to the point that an argument erupts has lost sight of the reality that his main goal is to sell the customer an automobile.

"Nothing is ever gained by winning an argument and losing a customer."

—C. F. Norton

We have all heard the phrase, "The customer is always right." As wrong as this may seem, it never helps the process of negotiations to prove that a customer is wrong, no matter how wrong they may be. This will only serve a purpose if you are trying to anger or embarrass him or her. After all, who isn't embarrassed when made to look unknowledgeable?

Disagreeing creates a combative atmosphere, an environment of one-upmanship between you and the customer, and you want them to work with you not against you. Many times I have heard a salesperson tell customers, "Your trade is not worth $10,000. It's only worth $8,000." At this point, the customers feel as though they are being challenged. Their first reaction to this situation will be to prove that the salesperson is wrong. The way they most commonly accomplish this is by taking their business to someone who will give them more for their vehicle and help them prove you wrong. Whether they get that amount for their vehicle or not, the end result is that you ultimately lose because they took their business elsewhere.

"He who has learned to disagree without being disagreeable has discovered the most valuable secret of a diplomat."

—Robert Estabrook

You will find it is always better to agree with the customer at least in some aspect and then elaborate on the subject. Since most customers may have already placed you in the role of adversary, the last thing you want to do is reinforce their belief by taking a view that is oppositional. Try doing the opposite of what they expect you to do.

A technique that many professional negotiators find effective is to agree with your customers, at least on some aspect of what they have said, and then proceed by elaborating on the subject further.

Beautiful

Example

"I agree with you completely, and I would probably feel the same way you do if I thought I wasn't getting enough for my vehicle. Keep in mind, however, that based on auction reports this is an amount that the used-car manager feels he would have to pay to obtain a vehicle of similar quality to yours if he bought it at the auction."

By doing this, you are not disagreeing. Furthermore, you are lending credibility to the number you presented. You are justifying the amount offered for their trade.

"Tact is the knack of making a point without making an enemy."

—Isaac Newton

Control Your Ego

In the process of negotiations, your ego can become your biggest enemy. It is something you need to leave behind when you walk away from your fellow salespeople. Too often in this busi-

* Clean Transition out

ness, negotiations collapse because the salesperson involved in the negotiations lets his or her ego get in the way.

I have found this occurs more frequently with experienced salespeople than it does with one who recently began selling cars. The more experienced salesperson knows that everything has been done correctly throughout the sales process and deserves the customer's business. She has helped the customer select the perfect vehicle. She has properly contended with all of the customer's objections. She has justified her position during negotiations. But the customers still want more. They want another concession. It may even be something very minor, such as two new tires or a bed liner. Why do they want it? Maybe the customers feel it is necessary to justify the purchase. Maybe they just want to walk away feeling as though they have won. At this point, the salesperson knows it is all about who gets the better of whom and, as a result, may become unwilling to yield. After all, how could she give in to yet another demand and still save face? Her ego won't allow her to admit defeat, even if it means she will lose the deal. Pride forces her to win the battle, yet lose the war. Always remember that negotiations are not about your pride; they are about coming to agreeable terms with your customer and selling a car, even if it means you must put your ego to the side and swallow your pride.

The Customer as a Negotiator

"If you wish to please people, you must begin by understanding them."

—Charles Reade

Each time you sit down at the table to negotiate, you will face a different customer with a unique personality or set of circumstances. No two people are exactly the same, and as a result no two customers will negotiate in the exact same manner. Nonetheless, you will begin to notice that customers will approach the negotiation process displaying similar, if not predictable, behavior. The reason for this is that while each customer is different as an individual, the factors that are motivating his or her actions are not. Once you learn to identify the type of negotiator you are facing, you gain insight into the customer's motivations and the best way to approach the negotiating table.

"Dogs bark at a person whom they do not know."

—Heraclitus

Identifying Your Type of Customer

- **The "Lay Down"**
- **The Bully**
- **Mr. Good Deal**
- **The "Take It or Leave It"/Wasn't Meant to Be**

The "Lay Down"

The "lay down" is the easiest type of customer to negotiate with. Even though I regard the use of this term when referring to an agreeable customer as derogatory, it is so commonly used throughout the car business that I will employ it simply for means of common familiarity. What is a "lay down?" It is a good customer that comes in and sees the value in you and what you are selling and respectively has no problem paying for the true value of your goods and services.

Most salespeople perceive this type of customer as less informed than all other types of buyers. Some may be, but this is not always the case. Sometimes they are just as informed about all of the important aspects of buying an automobile as the other types of buyers you encounter. However, they are more concerned with the relationship that is being established between themselves and the dealership or salesperson. This type of customer may not come right out and tell you, "I expect to be treated special." They are more concerned with being made to feel important to you and your business than they are in buying your vehicle and making sure you don't make a penny in the process.

Deep down, most customers are "lay downs." At least they are in every other buying environment they encounter. Consider for a moment how many consumers actually negotiate the price of groceries or the cost of a meal at a restaurant. The difference is that when the door to the kitchen swings shut at the restaurant, we do not hear the waiter who took our order laughing with and giving high-fives to the cook because he just sold a six-dollar cut of meat with a side of mashed potatoes for the full list price of twenty-eight dollars. The waiter is smart enough to know that what the customer is really paying for is service. They want to be made to feel special—just like our customers.

Because of scenarios similar to the one above, as automotive salespeople we, and those before us, have made it unthinkable for most of our customers to pay list price or MSRP for a vehicle when they visit a dealership. After all, would you feel comfortable paying $28.00 for another steak if you were made to feel foolish the last time you bought one? I doubt it.

That is why, when you are fortunate enough to encounter a customer who puts up very little resistance at the negotiating table, you must understand that their willingness to buy from you may be their way of saying, "I see the value in what you are offering, and I am willing to pay for it."

The most common example of this can be seen when examining the dealer-customer relationship found in many highline dealerships. People who walk in the showroom to buy a Mercedes or Jaguar value the treatment they receive from the dealership and how importantly they are made to feel throughout the experience—even if it means they must pay a little more to get it. I am not saying that every customer who walks into a highline dealership is a complete "lay down," but most value the relationship they have with a store and the service they expect to receive as much as, if not more than, the price alone.

If you and your dealership made the people visiting it feel like they meant everything in the world to you, then maybe you would discover a few more "lay downs." At the very least, you will keep these valuable customers returning to you and your store over and over again. They may even bring you some referrals; after all, the customers referred to as "lay downs" are typically your most satisfied customers.

The Bully

The bully is considered by many salespeople to be the complete opposite of the "lay down" and, as such, is perceived to be the most difficult to deal with. This could not be further from the truth. The bully is simply a "lay down" in disguise. This customer may have once been a "lay down" and still has ill feelings toward the entire car business because she feels wronged by it and is now seeking revenge. In the past, she was the customer that ordered the twenty-eight-dollar filet mignon with a side of mashed potatoes and even upgraded by ordering the seven-dollar piece of cheesecake—only to be left feeling empty when finding out that her waiter was more concerned with celebrating and giving high-fives to everyone at the restaurant than he was with making sure the customer was happy throughout the entire experience.

This type of customer can be easily recognized by his or her comments, which will begin soon after the meet and greet. These comments may include, but are not limited to, "I'll give you one shot at earning my business, so just go get me your best price right away, or I am out of here." Or you may even recognize the customer as a self-confessed, rehabilitated "lay down" when he or she announces, "I know how you guys operate. I have been screwed over by a car salesman before."

Once you begin to realize that the bully is only using these aggressive tactics as a defense mechanism, you soon begin to understand that this close cousin of the "lay down" is just looking for recognition or a feeling of importance through a different means. The bully truly seeks recognition for his knowledge and the respect he feels he rightfully deserves. If you have a hard time believing this, then carefully observe the next time you sell to a person exhibiting the characteristics of a bully. The minute the negotiations are over, he will begin to open up in hopes of building the relationship with you that he truly desires. I have even witnessed the air coming right out of him as he finishes signing the purchase order. He will exhale, his shoulders will relax, and he may even begin to smile and joke with you. He may even remark, "Yeah, I bet I am the most difficult person you have ever had to deal with," in an almost apologetic way.

Although these people may not be the easiest to contend with from the onset, I have found there are definitely a right way and a wrong way to deal with them. I suggest a three-step process to help lower their defenses.

Three-Step Process

1. An apology for the way they have been treated in the past.

2. An acknowledgment of their situation and assurance it won't happen again.

3. An expression of genuine interest in them and for their concerns.

Will this technique work on every customer? Will any technique work on every customer? The answer, of course, is no. However, if you at least take the time to address the customer's situation and begin building a relationship with him or her, you will dramatically improve your chances of converting a bully into a new sale and possibly even into a long-time loyal customer.

Mr. Good Deal

Mr. Good Deal is probably the most common type of customer you will encounter during your career selling cars. This type of customer focuses on one aspect of the car buying process: the money. These customers may view you and your dealership as inconsequential to the entire process. With this being the case, they approach what they consider the game of negotiating in an analytical, money-is-the-only-thing-that-matters fashion. You will recognize them instantly when they begin reciting canned phrases such as, "I am shopping around, so just give me your best price," and, "Tell me your best price, and then I will think about it and let you know."

Many dealerships try anything to avoid giving these customers a price or payment. I have even witnessed dealerships that let these customers leave without giving them a bit of information because they would not commit to buying immediately. For some reason, these salespeople and dealerships are under the impression that if they don't give customers what they want, then they will have a better chance of getting them back when they are ready to buy. The truth of the matter is that they are demonstrating their willingness to buy from you when they walk in the door. This technique of withholding information that some dealerships employ only works to ensure that the customer buys from someone else. Sometimes the customer leaves so irritated because of an inability to get information that it is almost a guarantee he or she will never consider your dealership as a place to do business now or in the future.

Overload Them with Information

You will probably find that the best way to increase your chances with customers such as this is to provide them with the information they are requesting and offer to give them more than they are expecting. If they ask for your best price, offer to give them an estimate for their trade as well. If they ask to see what their payment would be on a five-year loan, show them a payment for a four-, five-, and six-year loan. If you overload these customers with information, you will demonstrate your desire to work with them in a straightforward manner and gain their respect for your willingness to deal openly. It may be such a refreshing change from what they have experienced at other dealerships that they decide to buy from you right then and there. Additionally, the further you progress with these customers into the discussion of the monetary aspect of the deal, the closer you will come to selling them a car. After all, who buys a car without knowing this information anyway?

Keep Building Relationships

While these customers approach the process of negotiations as an analytical game of you against them, they are still human. The more time you spend with them, the more of a chance you have to build a relationship and establish a common ground with them. Hence, you increase your chances of getting them to like you and wanting to do business with you. Do not let their cold and calculated demeanors fool you into thinking you should forego making an attempt at building relationships with them. Sure, you might have to work extra hard at it, but in the long run you will be rewarded because they will become some of your most faithful customers. They will refer friends and family members, and more importantly they will come back to your store to see you because you not only gave them a good deal but also refused to let their conduct get in the way of establishing a relationship.

The "Take It or Leave It"

The "take it or leave it" customer is the closest thing you can find to the complete opposite of the "lay down." This type of customer displays complete indifference to the entire car-buying process and can be the most difficult to motivate into acting emotionally.

Some of you may disagree and believe that the customer who is angry or displays signs of hostility (the bully) is the opposite of a "lay down." Along these same lines of thinking, if I were to ask you what is the opposite of love, you might respond by telling me that hate is the opposite. As far as the dictionary definitions are concerned, you would be accurate. However a friend of mine once brought to my attention that as long as his ex-wife was breaking things and screaming at him there was still an emotional connection between the two and a chance that things would work out between them. It wasn't until she showed complete indifference that he realized the relationship was over. She no longer got mad at him because she didn't care one way or the other about him.

With this type of customer, it is very difficult to gain any type of negotiating leverage unless the wall they are putting up is hiding their true emotions and is merely their way of dealing with the situation at hand. You may find this to be the case in most instances.

The biggest mistake I see salespeople make when dealing with this type of customer is that they stop being salespeople. Not only do they stop trying to establish rapport, they cease trying to become involved with the customer emotionally. They stop selling their product and themselves. These salesmen believe the customer when he or she says, "If it is meant to be, it is meant to be." The salesperson lets this one line close them on the fact that this person has no emotional connection to purchasing a vehicle and gives up. Don't fall victim to this one-liner. Say to yourself, "If it's meant to be, it's up to me." Don't give up. Sell harder. Find something that will get the customer motivated. Customers are in your store for a reason. Remember, if they were completely happy with their present state of affairs regarding their current vehicles, they would not be in your dealership.

Third-Party Negotiators

Third-party negotiators—or "third-base coaches," as we like to refer to them in this business—have probably caused the breakdown of more negotiations than any other participants in the negotiation process. The reason is quite simple: they have no emotional involvement in the transaction. Furthermore, the third-party negotiator's sole motivation is rooted in the importance he or she derives from advising others on how to conduct their affairs. As we discussed earlier in chapter five, human beings have a deep-rooted need to feel important, and nothing feeds this need more than someone who is looking to you for direction.

Over the years, I have seen many salespeople become frustrated when they have a good prospect in front of them and a "third-base coach" that keeps putting up unnecessary roadblocks to the sale. When faced with this situation, many salespeople will attempt to go head-to-head with the advisors and say something to discredit them or discount their importance to the decision-making process. Many salespeople would love to look at the "third-base coaches" the moment they throw up a roadblock and ask, "Just what part of this transaction are you going to be helping with? The monthly payment or the down payment?" But we all know that this is the most counterproductive approach you can take because the part of the transaction they are helping with is the decision-making part.

Whether the "third-base coach" is your potential client's mother, brother, sister, girlfriend, boyfriend, pastor, coworker, or respected friend, you must resist the urge to discount the coach's importance and try instead to win him or her over to your way of thinking. That's right: put them to work *for* you instead of against you. If you can accomplish this task, you will have strengthened your position at the negotiating table.

To do this, you must be proactive in involving the "third-base coach" early in the sales process. Sell to both parties involved. Build a relationship and establish a rapport with both the buyer and the coach. After all, the reason your potential customer has brought a coach along is because he or she values the advice. The customer trusts the coach. Once negotiations begin, the coach who likes you and trusts you will become your biggest supporter. You may even have one or two that close the deal for you.

CHAPTER TEN

NEGOTIATIONS:
METHODS AND PRINCIPLES

In the past, salespeople were valued for the information, education, and products they brought to the buying public. Salespeople traveled from town to town and door to door introducing new products, new features, the benefits of those features, and the ways the consumers' lives would be enhanced by owning these items. Today, however, many consumers intentionally seek out and gather their own information from many different sources long before they ever enter a retail establishment or consider making a purchase.

As discussed earlier, this too is true regarding the automobile industry. Potential buyers may research the reputation of a product, its reliability rating, price comparisons with similar models, and much more before they ever consider buying a vehicle. They may have read automotive magazines and car reviews in their local newspaper or searched the Internet to arm themselves with every imaginable bit of information they could find about the vehicle they are interested in buying. Even if they haven't intentionally sought out information about your product or our industry, they have surely seen a television show revealing the inner workings of a dealership or portraying a bad image of the automotive business. At the very least, even the uninformed buyer has been bombarded with marketing on the television and radio to ensure that the first time they hear about your product is rarely when you speak of it. This abundance of information in today's market diminishes not only the customer's perceived value of the salesperson to the entire automobile-buying experience but also the negotiating leverage salespeople of years past enjoyed. This is not to say that as an automotive salesperson you no longer have advantages during the negotiation process with your customers. However, gone are the days when consumers felt they needed a salesperson to buy a car. As a salesperson, there are still advantages from which you may benefit.

Advantages

- Familiarity with your surroundings
- Control of the environment
- Access to more information and equipment
- You negotiate every day
- You have backup close by

Familiarity with Your Surroundings

Every day you go to work at the same dealership, sit at the same desk surrounded by the same people, and know the location of everything you need to sell a car. You are familiar with your environment, so familiar in fact that you can probably sit at your desk, close your eyes, and reach for a pen to write with or open your drawer and grab a worksheet from its location purely from memory. You possibly could pull every piece of paperwork you need to sell a car out of your files without even looking. This familiarity is an advantage for you. It is an advantage because you are in your comfort zone and can focus on the task at hand rather than trying to adjust to your surroundings. You can focus on selling, negotiating, and closing a car deal.

The customers, on the other hand, are not in their comfort zones. They are in strange territory, and something as simple as going to the bathroom requires your direction. Every action they make involves thought. Each time they have to think about what they are doing and how they are going to do it, they are not focusing on negotiating with you. They are distracted. This, for you, is like having the home-team advantage.

Control of the Environment

Not only are you familiar with your environment but you are in control of it. You are in control of the room temperature, the lighting, the seating, the music that is being played over the speakers, and much more. You are in control of the entire atmosphere.

At first this seems like a minor point. However, when negotiating, these little things matter. You may be sitting in a comfortable padded chair while your customer is sitting on a hard plastic or cold metal seat. You are listening to music that you enjoy while your customers may find it just slightly annoying because they can't concentrate with it playing. You enjoy the temperature at exactly seventy degrees while your customers may be more comfortable if it were set around three degrees lower due to their extra clothing. You could sit for hours and negotiate. Meanwhile, they feel an urgency to get on with business so they can get to a more comfortable environment; hopefully, this is in the seat of their new car.

Equally true is the reality that if your customer is too uncomfortable then you might just lose a sale because of it. You want your customer to be uncomfortable to the point where they will be motivated to proceed with negotiations but comfortable enough that they do not want to leave your dealership.

Access to More Information and Equipment

This home-team advantage extends to more aspects than just your familiarity and comfort with your environment. It also includes the fact that you have all the necessary equipment and information you need to identify your exact position when negotiating. Your dealership has books or computers for you and your managers to reference for the customer's trade-in value, the cost of the vehicle your customer is purchasing, the best interest rates available for financing a car, and all of the rebates and incentives that are available. With this being the case, you have more information available to you than the customer; furthermore, it is readily available for you to access as necessary.

Conversely, once your customer arrives at your dealership to negotiate, they are limited to the information that they can produce from memory or that they brought with them. Some customers may go so far as to print out copies of the research they have prepared and bring it with them to your dealership. Perhaps they even arm themselves with a calculator to help with the math. However, you will find most customers don't even bring so much as a paper or pen with which to write. This presents a clear disadvantage for your customers. As the saying goes, "Knowledge is power," and this is true regarding the advantage you possess by having all the equipment and information you need readily available to use as you wish.

You Negotiate Every Day

Your customer may buy a car once every few years. You, on the other hand, sit face-to-face every day with one or more customers negotiating prices, trade values, payments, and finance terms. You are a professional negotiator, and you practice your craft every day. This experience alone affords you a clear advantage.

You Have Backup Close By

Sometimes the process of negotiating a car deal can continue for hours. With this being the case, you may find that at times your energy, patience, or ideas are wearing thin. You may not be able to come to terms with your customer. However, you have one last chance: the "turnover." The "turnover," commonly referred to among sales professionals as a "TO," is when you introduce another salesperson or one of your managers into the negotiation process. The TO allows you the advantage of presenting a fresh new face to the negotiations when you find that the process is not advancing in the fashion you expected.

Many times when you reach the point where you feel you have been negotiating too long and have reached a point where negotiations have all but broken down, chances are the customer in front of you is feeling the same way. When you introduce the TO into the situation, you are creating an advantage for your side in two ways: you are providing a fresh perspective and allowing the customer to save face.

The Advantages of the TO

- **Brings a fresh perspective**

A new face brings a fresh perspective to the table. This fresh perspective that the person you turned over the deal to may be just the thing your customer needs to justify the purchase, and they will finalize the deal.

- **Allows the customer to save face**

Consider for a moment that your customers have been telling you for hours that they will not pay more than three hundred dollars a month; yet at the end of negotiations, you are still twenty-dollars-a-month away from a deal. At this point, your customer is either forced to walk away from the deal or go against the amount they stated they would not go above. They have to retreat on their offer. For some customers, their pride will not allow this. This is when the person you TO your deal to can make a huge difference. Your customers have not been telling the TO that they would not pay a penny over three hundred dollars a month. For this reason, your customers don't need to worry about what the TO will think if they compromise their position to put a deal together. This allows your customers to save face. Always remember that bringing another party into the negotiations may give your customers the ability to change their minds without affecting their egos.

- **Sends a signal that the negotiation process is nearing the end**

The customers you deal with know that when you bring in someone else, you have done all that you can do. They sense that you have exhausted all of your options, and so now they must talk to someone else. Subconsciously, this will send the signal that if they are going to make a concession to try to put a deal together, now is the time. It also makes them feel as though they have done a thorough job at negotiating. Believe it or not, there are some customers who will not finalize a deal with the first person they talk to because they believe they won't get their best deal until they speak with the "big boss," as some of them refer to the TO.

As you can see from the examples above, car salespeople still have many advantages when negotiating a car deal. Keep them in mind, and utilize them to the best of your ability.

The Higher Authority

With all of these advantages that dealerships and their salespeople benefit from by simply possessing the home team advantage during the negotiation process, one might think that there is no need for anything more. This, however, is not true. In the automobile business, you can never have too much of an advantage. For this reason, most dealerships structure the sales staff to afford themselves another big advantage during the negotiating process.

This structure employs the salesperson as an intermediary between the potential customer and the dealership's decision maker, which in most cases is the sales management. With this being the case, the salesperson is afforded the benefit of having a built-in higher authority (sales management) to draw from when confronted by their customers during the negotiation process. The fact that the manager is the true decision maker for the dealership is the salesperson's "out" during the negotiations.

In theory, this is much the same as a customer saying, "I need to talk to my wife," in an attempt to use his spouse as an "out" when confronted by a salesperson seeking a commitment to buy. The use of a higher authority by both buyers and sellers is quite commonplace in daily life as well as in today's market throughout any industry you may examine.

The act of referring to another entity as the decision maker is seen in almost every aspect of our daily lives. It allows one negotiating party to gain information about the other party's position without committing to a particular situation or needing to make a decision. Anyone who has tried direct sales to a business entity knows what it is like to hear, "You can just leave your proposal with me, and I will run it by the boss (or board of directors)." Or maybe you are one of the millions who has sub-mitted a loan application to a bank employee who you believed had the power to approve your loan only to hear, "Well, every-thing on the application looks fine. All I need to do now is fax it over to the vice president of the bank to get the final approval."

Whether you realize it or not, the higher-authority concept has been used on every one of us since childhood. After all, who as a child has not asked one parent a question only to hear them exclaim, "You need to ask your father," who then counters with, "It's up to your mother."

As you can tell by the examples above, there is nothing exclu-sive to car dealers regarding the implementation of the higher-authority method. Actually, I would even be willing to bet that if we could look back in time and see which party—the customer or the salesperson—used this method first, we would find that a customer resorted to the use of a higher authority years before any salesperson or dealership ever thought of it.

Positions of Power at the Negotiating Table

You only win when the customer feels he or she has won.

Every time negotiations occur, each party is negotiating from a different position of power. If you are offering a product or service that is in limited quantity yet in high demand, you are negotiating from a position of power. With the exception of a few uncommon instances, you will find that as an automobile salesperson this will rarely be the case for you. As they say in real estate, it is a buyer's market. There are an abundance of new and used automobiles available for sale, and consumers know it.

Because of this, consumers are the ones negotiating from a position of power. They know that they can get up and walk out on any of your offers and be in another dealership, negotiating for a similar vehicle with someone else, within fifteen minutes.

As a result, most consumers use this leverage to negotiate their deal until they feel as though they have reached a point where they are in a win-lose situation. Win for them; lose for you and the dealership. In a perfect world, every deal would be consummated when it is a win-win situation for both parties. In this business, that would equate to you selling a car and making a good commission, and the customer getting a fair discount as well as a new vehicle. This is not, however, a perfect world, and win-win is not good enough for many customers. Many customers feel as though they have to get the better of the car salesman before they are willing to consummate a deal.

Does this sound a little cynical? Of course it does, but it is the truth. Many customers you meet negotiate motivated by the larceny in their hearts. Good negotiators understand this and have the ability to make a customer feel as though he or she is in a win-win situation early on in the process. They also understand that the sooner the customer feels he or she is winning, the more profit they will make on the deal.

This is the element of negotiating that differentiates the salesman making a six-figure income from the one earning only enough to keep above the poverty level but selling the same number of cars as the salesperson who is prospering. The six-figure salesman knows how to make the customer feel like a winner faster.

This may be one of the most elementary aspects of negotiating and one that most salespeople understand right from the very beginning. They know customers must feel like they are winning before they are willing to consummate a deal. I understood this after only a brief time in the car business. However, it wasn't until I was working with one particular customer that the power this aspect of the negotiating process possessed became clear to me.

The customer I am referring to came into our dealership and immediately asked me what his trade-in was worth. At this point, he hadn't even picked out a vehicle. He only wanted to know the value of his trade. I responded by explaining that I would need to get the used-car manager to take a look at his car and would do so as soon as we had picked out a vehicle for him. After all, as far as I was concerned, if he wasn't buying one of our cars, then he wasn't trading but rather selling, and our dealership doesn't buy cars like the one he owned.

My offer to get his vehicle appraised after selecting a vehicle to purchase was not good enough for him. He then persisted, "Well, what do you think it is worth?" Instinctively, I remarked (knowing the answer I would get) after looking out the window at his ten-year old car, "I'm not sure. I don't appraise vehicles. What would you sell something like that for in the newspaper—three thousand, maybe thirty-five hundred dollars?" (I knew this is what most people think their old cars are worth.) His response to this was, "Yeah, I was only thinking twenty-five hundred, but if they are crazy enough to give me that amount, I'd buy a car today."

I could see by the look in his eyes that he thought I was inexperienced and a fool for telling him that his car could be worth the amount I had stated. Three minutes into the sales process, this customer was so sure that he had tricked a green salesperson into doing something stupid that he couldn't wait to select the vehicle he was going to buy. As far as he was concerned, he was already a winner—so much so that when he went out and selected a low mileage, two-year-old vehicle on our lot, he never even stopped to ask the price. (Our cars didn't have prices on them.) But he didn't care. He wanted too much for his trade, and he thought he found just the fool to give it to him. The larceny in this customer's heart blinded him into believing that he was in a winning situation for himself and a losing situation for the dealership, and he couldn't sign the paperwork fast enough.

It would be nice if it worked this way with every customer. However, each customer is different and will feel as though he or she is getting the best of you and your dealership at a different stage in the negotiations. It is your job to get your customer to this point as quickly as possible.

"Diplomacy is the art of letting someone else have your way."

—Daniele Vare, Italian diplomat

Parameters for the Negotiations

During the tenure of your career selling cars, you will encounter many different types of customers and scenarios. With this being the case, it is advisable to try to establish some ground rules to help improve your chances at the negotiating table. This may not be necessary to do with every customer you encounter; however, you will have many experiences where you will find this practice to be useful to the negotiation process.

Ground Rules

- Identify or determine the parties involved in the negotiations.

- Agree beforehand that it is not personal.

- Agree ahead of time that you may disagree on some points.

Parties Involved in the Negotiations

One of the most difficult situations that you may encounter when trying to sell and negotiate a car deal occurs when you are confronted with a situation in which there are too many people involved in the transaction. At some point, you will be working with a customer and his or her significant other. Additionally, a friend and the friend's girlfriend or boyfriend may have decided to join the mix. Now you are faced with four people, all of whom have different opinions and may feel the need to be heard during one or more phases of the negotiation process. They will try to gang up on you; of course, the more people, the better the deal.

You will find that if you confront this situation early in the process, you will increase your chances of successfully negotiating a deal. *What* you say may not be as important as *when* you say it. If you wait until you are in the middle of negotiations to try to eliminate the non-decision-making party from the process, then you run the risk of insulting that party as well as your customer. Remember, the other party is the customer's friend or family member. Instead, address the situation as soon as you are able to.

During one of the phases leading up to negotiations, you may want to address the buyer by saying something such as, "You know you are going to have a difficult time buying a car today." Your customer, having never heard these words from a car salesperson before, will instinctively respond with something to the effect of, "Why's that?" At this point, you can address the situation. Tell them, "Well, I am a pretty good salesman, but even I know I can't convince four people to agree on all of the terms of buying one car. It's difficult enough with only one person." Most of the time, the parties unrelated to the transaction will interject by saying, "Oh, we don't have anything to do with the deal. We just came along because we had nothing better to do." Mission accomplished; they removed themselves from the process for you, and you have established who will be involved in the decision-making process.

Agree That It Is Not Personal

As many experienced salespeople reading this book know, some people take negotiations personally. You may show your customers a price or payment that is out of their budget, and they will lose control. They may stand up and threaten to leave your dealership. Maybe when you tell them what their trade is worth they will get mad and demand the keys to their trade back. They feel as though it is an attack on them rather than what it really is: an interaction between two parties in an attempt to come to agreeable terms on a situation.

If you are working with a customer that you feel may be like this, bring this point to his or her attention before the negotiations start, and you may just defuse a bomb before it goes off. Prior to presenting any numbers, say to your customer, "Some people buying cars tend to get offended during negotiations. If it's OK with you, I'd like us to agree that any numbers we discuss are just that, numbers on a page and nothing more, definitely nothing that either one of us should take personally or be insulted by. Is that fair enough for you?" Your customer will agree.

Agree to Disagree

Agreeing ahead of time that you and the customer may disagree on some points during negotiations will help you to establish an open path of communication between yourself and your potential customer. Consider that most customers are not trained professional negotiators like you, and for this reason, when they encounter a situation where they disagree with someone, they instinctively elevate the situation to a point of argument. This, of course, is the last thing you want to happen.

To prevent disagreements from happening, it is beneficial to address the possibility that you won't see eye to eye on every issue up front. With customers that you believe are argumentative, you may want to begin negotiations by preempting them with something such as, "Before we go over the numbers, if it is OK with you, I would like to agree that we may disagree on some points. If we come to a point that you don't agree with something, I would encourage you to share it with me. Does that sound fair enough to you?"

Some salespeople are afraid to do this because they feel as though they are inviting trouble. The reality of the situation is that your customer is probably going to disagree with you on some point anyway. What you are really inviting is for your customer to express personal concerns to you in an open, rational manner. Furthermore, you are opening the lines of communication.

Negotiating Principles

Up until now, we have examined the benefits of establishing some ground rules with your customer when negotiating. Remember from chapter nine, since you can't control all of your customer's actions, the biggest impact you can make on the negotiating process is to control your own. In the remainder of this chapter, we will examine some principles that you are completely in control of and that, if applied properly, will benefit you during the negotiation process.

Principles

- Try not to allow your customers to set their expectations too high.
- Do not let your expectations become too unrealistic.
- Do not get lured into one-sided negotiations.
- Never accept the first offer.
- Start with the highest possible figures.

Try not to allow your customers to set their expectations too high.

Consider yourself an expectation manager. The better you manage the expectations of your customer and follow through by meeting or exceeding them, the more successful you will become in negotiations. After all, it is every quality-oriented salesperson's mission to exceed customer expectations. This can be difficult since the automotive industry as a whole has employed advertising that instills unrealistic expectations in your customers' minds before they ever walk into your store. Unfortunately, this is something over which you have no control. However, you do have the ability to exercise some control over your customers' levels of expectation while they are at your dealership. Remember, people don't always get what they want, but they do get what they expect.

Do not let your expectations become too unrealistic.

Quite often, salespeople will fall into the trap of allowing their own expectations to get in the way of consummating a deal. Be careful that you don't fall into this trap. Every salesman would like to sell a car for a four- or five-thousand-dollar profit. However, you can't expect this—at least not every time. If you allow your expectations to become this unrealistic, you will find that you are losing more deals than you are making. Remember, pigs get fat, and hogs get slaughtered.

Instead, you should judge the success or failure of your deal based on how competently you perform given the circumstances you face. If you know that you have sold your product for the maximum amount possible to the customer you have in front of you, then you have conducted a successful negotiation no matter how much you profited. Consider this for a moment: if you are negotiating with a customer who has been informed as to the exact invoice amount of the vehicle you are selling, and they are only willing to pay you one hundred dollars above that amount regardless of the information they possess, then you have succeeded at negotiating a deal that results in a profit of five hundred dollars for your dealership. Although you didn't earn a profit of four or five thousand dollars, you did negotiate successfully. Your main intention when negotiating should be to maximize your profit with each individual customer. Negotiate the best deal you can with the customer you have in front of you, and don't let your expectations get the best of you.

Do not get lured into one-sided negotiations.

While many customers today expect to walk away from the negotiation process feeling as though they have won and that the dealership and salesperson have lost, this does not mean that you should allow the negotiation process to become completely one sided. To prevent this from happening, it is important that you do not make a concession without making a condition. If your customers ask you to compromise your position, you must ask for something in return. This condition can be something as simple as your customer's commitment to buy the vehicle if you make the concession they are requesting. If you fail to do this, you will be lessening the importance of any concession that you make. Furthermore, you are opening the door for one-sided negotiations to begin. If they ask and you give instinctively, they will want more. As long as you keep giving, they will keep asking for more. After all, you made it too easy the first time.

Never accept the first offer.

This is a lesson many salespeople in the car business learn the hard way. No matter how good a deal the customers' first offer is for you, and no matter how firm you think their offer is if you accept it, they will feel as though they left money lying on the table. They will feel as though they could have done a better job. If you make negotiations too easy for your customers, they will have second thoughts. They will automatically ponder the question, "Should we have asked for more of a discount?" This then leads to their assumption, "We should try again somewhere else and ask for a bigger discount." At this point, if your customers think they can save more money somewhere else, they will come up with every objection imaginable to back out of their commitment.

To prevent this from happening, you must counter their offer by asking for more. Whether it is a few hundred dollars more on the price, a couple dollars a month more on the payment, or a little more money down, you must ask for more. Whether you get it or not is not as important as the fact that you countered their offer. By presenting your customer with a counteroffer, you are conveying the message that they are negotiating a good deal. Even if they reject your counteroffer, you are still accomplishing the task of making your customers feel as though they have won, and furthermore you are preventing them from having second thoughts about their offer. You may even be surprised when they accept your counteroffer.

Start with the highest possible figures.

At auctions, bidding begins with a low figure, and participants bid against each other, raising their offers for the merchandise until someone emerges as the highest bidder. Unfortunately, or perhaps fortunately, you don't work at an auction. You work at a car dealership. You work at a retail establishment, and you can't start at the bottom and work your way up. You have to start at the top and work your way down.

With this being the case, it is to your advantage to start with the highest figures possible. Start with more than you ever expect to get. Many salespeople today have trouble doing this with every customer. Why? The answer is simple: they know they have sold similar vehicles for less to previous customers. This knowledge causes these salespeople to lower their own perceived value of the vehicles they are selling. This is also an example of lowering your expectations. Remember, the price where you begin negotiations and the price that the vehicle is ultimately sold for are normally not the same. The higher the beginning price, the more negotiating room you afford yourself, decreasing your chances of arriving at an impasse during the negotiation process.

Starting with the highest possible figures helps to shape your customers' perceived value of the vehicle they are buying. Your customers may never admit to you that the list price or MSRP is the true value of the vehicle they are negotiating to purchase. They may even claim it is ridiculous when you mention it. Nonetheless, it is still important for you to raise that perceived value in your customers' minds. The customer wants you to do it; after all, who hasn't heard a proud new owner discussing the value of the vehicle he recently purchased exclaiming, "The sticker price was twenty thousand dollars, but I got it for seventeen," or discussing the used car he purchased saying, "These cars sell for thirty-five thousand dollars brand new, but I got this one for only eighteen." This perceived value of the vehicle purchased is a source of pride for most consumers, who will admit it to everyone except the car salesman. If you don't start with the highest possible price, you are discounting the value of your vehicle and robbing your customer of his or her bragging rights. Remember, America may be the only place in the world where people take pride in bragging about how little they paid for their car and how much they paid for their home.

CHAPTER ELEVEN
THE TRADE-IN: VALUE VS. WORTH

"What is a cynic? A man who knows the price of everything and the value of nothing."

—Oscar Wilde

If there is any single element of the automotive-sales process that could be attributed to differentiating the car business and the way business is conducted from any business in the retail industry, it would surely be the fact that we in the automotive business are willing to accept a customer's current or used product in trade toward a new one. We are the only retail industry that as a general practice trades in our customers' old merchandise and gives them credit toward their new purchases. Surely, there are exceptions to this rule, but for the most part any other merchandise a customer owns must be sold by the consumer themselves in order for them to realize its value.

This practice of taking a customer's car in trade to aid in the sale of our vehicle can best be described as a necessary evil. It is necessary because it increases the number of people in the market that are able to purchase a vehicle from us; it is evil because of the complexities it creates for every other aspect of the sales process.

Reports show that more than half of all vehicle purchases involve customer trade-ins. Therefore, it should be clear to you that the better you become at addressing the issue of your customer's trade-in, the more success you will have selling cars. In the remainder of this chapter, we will examine the best ways for this to be accomplished.

To most Americans, the automobile has become more than just a mode of transportation; it has become an outward expression of their identities. Whether an economy car driven by the environmental activist, a red convertible sports car driven by the successful stockbroker, or a minivan driven by the soccer mom, the cars we own and drive announce to the world who we are. This is why it is so important for you to remember to be tactful when addressing the issue of your customer's trade-in. If not, you will run the risk of insulting your customer on a personal level.

During the course of the sale, a customer may tell you that her trade-in is a piece of junk, She may even claim to hate the vehicle entirely. She can because it is her right; after all, it is her car. If you criticize her vehicle, she will instinctively become defensive. This most commonly occurs during one of two phases of the sales process: either when the vehicle is being appraised or when its value is being discussed. Understand that these are the critical times in which you must proceed with caution and tact.

The Appraisal

If you have been in this business long enough, you know that getting your customer's vehicle appraised presents more of an opportunity to benefit the sales process than just simply obtaining a value for your customer's vehicle. It presents an opportunity for you to find out information about your customer and his or her motivations. In addition, the information you obtain can ultimately aid you in the negotiation process.

The Trade-In Evaluation Form

Most dealerships employ the use of some type of trade evaluation sheet to facilitate the process of gathering information regarding the vehicle that will potentially be traded in. When used properly, this form can be your biggest asset if you happen to reach a sticking point in the negotiation process. You must, however, use it as more than a place to document the vehicle information and current mileage. You must use it as the tool it has the potential to be.

You will notice that even a customer who is hesitant to open up and express his or her true wants, needs, and motivations will suddenly transform into a bundle of available information when you express an interest in his or her trade. The customer may not have more than two words to say to you throughout the entire sales process until you take out a trade evaluation sheet and start asking questions about the vehicle. Interestingly enough, customers will be more than happy to share any information with you that they think will increase the value of their vehicles.

In addition to the standard information your customer gives you about the vehicle (year, make, model, miles, and vehicle identification number), you should be sure to ask questions regarding its history. These questions should include whether routine maintenance has or has not been performed, how often the oil was changed, whether the vehicle has new tires or brakes, and if there have been any major cosmetic or mechanical repairs performed on the vehicle. Typically at this point, your customer will begin rattling off a list of everything ever done to the vehicle in an attempt to build its value. As he or she provides this information, be sure to write it all down on the trade-appraisal sheet. This information will not only serve to impress upon the used-car manager the true value of the vehicle, it will be documented on your evaluation form in black and white in case you need to reference it later.

Surely many of you are wondering how soliciting information from a customer that will help build value in the trade-in vehicle could benefit you at the negotiating table in the long run. The truth of the matter is that most customers will be more than willing to tell you about all of the money they have spent maintaining their cars and are hesitant to reveal any damages.

They will give you partial truths. Remember, each time they share with you all of the maintenance they have done to their cars, they are really revealing the amount of money they have spent to keep driving their old vehicles. As an example, if a customer has paid two hundred dollars for tires, two hundred dollars for an alternator, and two hundred dollars for a starter within just the past year, then she is really telling you that she pays an average of fifty dollars a month on repairs in addition to her monthly car payment.

In chapter seven, we used an example that demonstrates the usefulness of having this information when you are contending with a customer's objections to the payment. Here is the example again.

Example

Customer Objection: I can't afford payments of three hundred a month. I am only paying two hundred and fifty now, and I told you I didn't want my payment to go up.

Pause

Salesperson: I understand how you feel about making a payment of that amount. Other customers that I have dealt with in the past felt the exact same way as you at first until they found that by owning a new car with a warranty they would be saving enough on repairs to more than compensate for the additional fifty dollars a month they were spending for the new car.

Just consider for a moment, if you spent two hundred dollars on a set of new tires, two hundred dollars for a new alternator, and two hundred dollars for a starter, then you are spending six hundred dollars a year on repairs on top of the payment you are making each month; that averages out to about fifty dollars more a month just to drive your old car. In addition, add the amount you are paying the mechanic to the amount you are paying the bank, and you will find that you are already making a payment of three hundred a month; you just don't have the new car to show for it. Are you ready to start driving that new car you've been paying for all along?

To reiterate, it is always advantageous to have as much information about your customer's motivation and situation as possible before negotiations begin. Use your trade-evaluation form as a tool to help you gain this insight and not just as a place for the used-car manager to write what he feels about the value of this vehicle.

The Vehicle and the Silent Walk Around

Every day when you wake up, you probably shower, brush your teeth, comb your hair, and either shave if you are a man or put on makeup if you are a woman. When you do this, most of your time is spent looking in the mirror. Over the years, small changes will take place right in front of your eyes; there may be a few wrinkles here and there, or maybe a gray hair or two appears, and as time passes a few more of each emerge. You see these gradual changes taking place almost as if they are occurring in slow motion—so slowly that you don't even notice how differently you appear to the rest of the world. As far as you are concerned, you're the same person you were when you were eighteen years old, just modified a bit. To the rest of the world, you look entirely different—so different that when you run across someone you haven't seen in ten or twenty years, they barely recognize you. They may not even recognize you at all.

Why is this? Have you changed that much and failed to realize it? Yes, you have.

What, you may ask, does your appearance have to do with vehicles being traded in? This example helps to demonstrate the point that when you see something every day you begin to grow accustomed to the changes that are occurring gradually. You actually may even become blind to them. This same thing happens in the minds of your customers regarding their trade-ins. Despite the fact that a customer may have bought a brand-new car and driven it every day for the past ten years and that over time the car may have gotten a little door ding here and a bumped fender there, the upholstery is starting to show wear, there is a cigarette burn on the carpet, and one of the power windows stopped working a year ago, he perceives his car to be a good car in good condition. These are not the things that come to the forefront of your customer's mind when he thinks of his trade; after all, he doesn't look at the interior—he sits in it. And as for the rear window that doesn't go up or down, he never used it anyway. To your customer, this car is a vehicle he bought brand new and took good care of, and it never once left him stranded. He doesn't see its imperfections. This is the reason you need to bring to his attention that it is not the new car he purchased years ago, free of any imperfections, as in his mind's eye. It is a ten-year-old vehicle that shows considerable wear and tear with dents and dings and wouldn't be considered a retail vehicle in most markets because it has close to 200,000 miles on it. To present the reality of the car, you must be tactful in order not to insult your customer. This is where the "silent walk around" comes into play.

The "silent walk around" is a technique that helps to depreciate the customers' perceived value of their trade-in in a tactful manner. Remember, sometimes your actions speak louder than your words. This is one of those instances.

To conduct the silent walk around, you simply ask your customer to accompany you to acquire the exact miles and vehicle identification number off of their trade-in. Once you get to the vehicle, you should begin your inspection at the front passenger side and proceed by walking around the car slowly. As you do this, you should be sure to touch any imperfections the car has such as dents, dings, and areas of faded paint or rust; however, there is no need for you to comment on them—just touch them or lightly brush over them with your hand. This is the silent aspect of the appraisal. Silent does not mean you shouldn't say a single word to your customer at any point; it simply means you shouldn't make comments about the defects in the vehicle. By merely touching the imperfections you find, you are bringing them to your customers' attention, thus conveying the message that their vehicle is not quite as perfect as believed. Most customers will even make a comment in defense of the imperfection you have brought to their attention. For instance, if you touch a dent, they will probably say something such as, "Someone backed out on me in the parking lot of the supermarket."

After working your way around the vehicle, silently acknowledging any flaws on the exterior, you should arrive at the front driver's side where you will now be able to copy the vehicle's identification number off of the dashboard. Most dealerships require you to obtain this information directly off of the car. After you have completed this, ask your customer if he or she would mind looking into the vehicle to tell you the exact number of miles on the odometer; this serves to bring the true number of miles on the vehicle to his or her attention, as well as to give you the exact information you need. Believe it or not, many customers don't know how many miles there are on their cars.

If you find yourself dealing with a customer that is trading a high-mileage vehicle and who is under the impression the car is still worth an unrealistic amount of money, it can be helpful to emphasize the number of miles the odometer has accumulated. This can be done in a very subtle and lighthearted manner by commenting something to the effect of, "Wow, you sure get every penny's worth out of your cars, don't you?" when they tell you the number of miles on the vehicle. This statement is normally taken by most customers as a compliment, and they counter it with prideful responses such as, "I sure do." Subliminally, this admission will help them to realize that the more value they have taken out of a vehicle, the less it could be worth.

Next, you will want to proceed by inspecting the interior of the vehicle. Check all of the accessories such as the radio, air conditioner, blinkers, lights, power seat, mirrors, and windows to make sure they are in working order. Similar to the earlier example interaction between you and your customer regarding the dent, when you attempt to put down a power window that is inoperable, your customer will probably make a comment to defend the broken window such as, "That just stopped working a while back, and since I never used it, I didn't see a need to get it repaired." Again, he is making a mental note of how his "cream puff" is not as perfect as he thought when he arrived at your store.

This process can take a bit more time than just leaving your customer sitting in the showroom while you go out by yourself to get the miles and vehicle identification number; however, it is much more effective than waiting until the negotiations have begun to address the vehicle's true condition. Nevertheless, the small things you do leading up to the negotiation process determine whether you spend 20 percent or 80 percent of your time negotiating. You decide!

The Trade Value

What is my car worth? The answer to this question alone has probably sent more potential deals into a tailspin at a crucial time than any other single question you will encounter in the negotiation process. How do you tell someone that her five-hundred-dollar car is not worth the three thousand she believes it is worth without insulting her? Worse yet, how do you tell someone who owes the bank twenty thousand on his current vehicle that it is only appraised for *fifteen* thousand?

Each dealership you work for will take its own approach to structuring the numbers for your initial presentation to the customer. Some will hold back on the trade value initially so they can give more to the customer if necessary. Some dealerships start deals by allowing the customer more for the trade to appease him or her from the beginning. Some may not even address the exact value of the trade and attempt to avoid the subject by writing, "Pay off your trade," on the worksheet that is presented. However the dealership you work for decides to address the trade-in on your worksheet, there will be many times in your career when a customer looks at you and asks point-blank, "How much are you giving me for my car?" This is the point when you have to break the news. I say "break the news" because rarely has a customer exclaimed, "Wow, that's more than I ever thought my car was worth!" after hearing the used-car manager's version of the value for the trade-in. Actually, quite the opposite normally happens. Some of your customers may actually get mad or insulted when they learn the amount of their appraisal. Why do they get mad? Typically, most customers determine unrealistic values for their trades, which they have derived from misinformation encountered on a regular basis. If they see a ten-year-old car for sale on the side of the road that is similar to theirs with "$3000" written across the windshield, they register this information in their minds and deduce that their cars must be worth at least that amount. They may even skim through the classified ads in the newspaper or on the Internet and find a vehicle that is the same year, make, and model as theirs advertised for thirty-five hundred dollars or best offer; this adds yet another confirmation to their beliefs that the vehicles they own are worth a considerable amount of money. To top it all off, your customers have decided that before coming to your dealership, they are going to do some "real" research on the values of their vehicles and proceed by getting on the Internet and searching Web sites until they find one that says their cars are worth as much as they want them to be worth. The problem with this approach is that the information they are gathering from these sources does not give an accurate account of the market value of their vehicles. Remember, rule number one regarding the value of anything is, "Something is only worth as much as someone is willing to pay for it." It's not worth what a buyer's guide says it is worth or the amount others wish they could sell theirs for. This is where many of your customers get their information.

This issue of the trade-in is the reason customers will become disappointed, offended, mad, upset, insulted, or disgusted when you tell them what the dealership is willing to give them for their vehicles. After all, they have three other sources of information that helps support their versions of the "true" values of their vehicles. This leads to the conclusion that it must be that the dealership is trying to steal their trade-ins. Now they become angry. It is the customer who has set his or her expectations too high based on misinformation. This puts you in a kettle of soup; it becomes your job to get your customer to accept the true worth of his or her vehicle—that is, if you want to make a sale. In order to do this, you must justify your numbers.

Each person you encounter will respond to the trade in a different way. A person might be shocked when you tell him the value of his trade and will exclaim, "You're kidding me! My car has got to be worth more than that." Another will deny that the amount could possibly be accurate and declare, "I can sell my car on the side of the road for at *least* three thousand bucks." Some customers will instantly become angry; many more will try to bargain with you and demand more money for their trades. All of these responses are natural—so natural and common, in fact, that psychologists from the University at Buffalo (buffalo.edu) have identified a series of steps that people experience emotionally in order to cope with disappointing events in their lives. It is referred to as the grieving process. While many of us instantly associate the word "grieving" with death, the process they have identified can actually be applied to many disappointing situations. When you break the news to your customers that their cars are not worth what they think, they may experience a sense of loss. This may trigger the grieving process. If you understand this process, you will be more prepared to deal with a customer who is experiencing it.

The Grieving Process

- **Stage One—Shock**

  Your customer may respond out of complete surprise with a statement like, "You're kidding me! My car has got to be worth more than that."

- **Stage Two—Denial**

  Your customer refuses to accept the information you have given and may even state, "I can't believe that my car is only worth…"

- **Stage Three—Anger**

  Your customer will respond either by withdrawing from interaction with you or will show outward signs of annoyance. He or she may respond with a statement such as, "You've got to be out of your mind! That's ridiculous! I'm insulted."

- **Stage Four—Bargaining**

  Your customer will attempt to make a deal with you to change the current information he is facing. He may say something to the effect of, "Well, I want three thousand for my trade, and if they give me that much I will buy the new car."

- **Stage Five—Depression**

  Many customers will not say much at this point. They may just sit with blank looks on their faces, pondering their situations. This phase occurs most commonly when bargaining has not improved their situations. They may try to bargain again or revert back to anger.

- **Stage Six—Acceptance**

   Your customer finally comes to terms with the reality of the situation and decides that it is time to move on.

   Each customer you contend with will begin this process at a different stage. As you know, there are no two people who are exactly alike, and everyone responds to situations differently. Regardless of the stage where your customer starts in the process, it is your job to get him or her to accept the reality as quickly and easily as possible. It is your job to get him or her to the point of acceptance.

   While performing the silent walk around may help you prepare some of your customers to accept the reality of what their vehicles are worth, you may still be faced with a customer in denial, and you have the task of delivering the unpleasant news. You will find that most of the time you can help to determine the stage of the grieving process where your customer starts or, at the very least, how quickly he or she progresses through the stages based on how you approach delivering this information. This may be the point at which salespeople create an unnecessary confrontation with the customer simply by choosing the wrong words to tell the customer what the trade-in vehicle is worth. Below is an example of a typical interaction between a customer and salesperson regarding the trade-in value.

Example #1

Customer: What is my car worth?

Salesperson: The appraised value of your vehicle is fifteen thousand dollars.

Customer: (Shock) You're kidding me; my payoff to the bank is twenty thousand dollars.

Salesperson: Well, the used-car manager appraised it, and he said it is only worth fifteen thousand, and he's been doing this for over twenty years.

Customer: (Denial) My car is worth more than fifteen thousand. **(Anger)** Your used-car manager is out of his mind. You guys are all crooks. Just get me the keys to my car.

As you can see, this customer started out in shock, then progressed to the denial stage, and ended up angry. At this point, many deals spiral out of control. Your customer is angry, and, when angry, people are normally not thinking rationally. If you are unable to give him the amount he wants for his trade, your chances of selling a car have all but ended; his anger is your enemy in this deal. It is not conducive to a productive negotiating environment, and typically your best efforts to justify your numbers at this point will not be well received by your customer.

Wouldn't it be nice if your customer could understand how you arrived at the figure for the trade and have no reason to be mad at you? The customer can—if you give some justification first. Below is an example of a way you can do this.

Example #2

Customer: What is my car worth?

Salesperson: Based on recent auction reports, the used-car manager could replace your vehicle for fifteen thousand dollars.

Customer: Are you trying to tell me that the value of my car is only fifteen thousand dollars?

Salesperson: That is the amount this dealership would expect to pay if it wanted to purchase a vehicle similar to yours through the auction or from one of its wholesalers.

Customer: I wouldn't take fifteen thousand for my car. At the last dealership, I was offered seventeen, plus I owe twenty to the bank.

Salesperson: I understand that. Suppose we would allow you the same amount for your trade here. Would you buy it now?

You should notice that this scenario played out entirely differently than the first example. Why? Justification was given. When you justify the number you are giving as you give it, you are defusing a bomb before it goes off. This helps to progress the customer past the stages of shock, denial, and anger, directly to the bargaining stage.

The salesperson in the second example made sure not to use words like "worth" or "value," unlike the salesperson in the first example. These words are too loosely defined, and it is easy to argue a point when the two parties are not even discussing the same subject. Remember that most misunderstandings result as a lack of understanding. Consider that if a customer uses the word "value" or "worth," he is referring to what he would expect to receive for that car if he sold it outright on the retail market. However, when a salesperson refers to the value of the customer's vehicle, he is referring to what it is worth to the dealership through the channels it has for obtaining one.

Once you have jumped all of the hurdles discussed in previous chapters, you are ready to move into the final phase of the deal. Don't think that at this point your work is done; it may have just begun. As with every phase of the process, there are different types of skills required to finalize different deals.

CHAPTER TWELVE
FINALIZING THE DEAL

"It takes time to succeed because success is merely the natural reward of taking time to do anything well."

—Joseph Ross

Whether it is the feeling of exhilaration the kicker gets from kicking a last-second field goal to win a football game in overtime or the sensation that comes from being the salesperson who says just the right thing at just the right time to finalize the deal with that impossible customer, nothing quite compares to the feeling you get when you are rewarded for the fruits of your labor with a victory. While the sales process is not about the salesperson winning and the customer losing, it is about you walking away from the table after having done the best job you can while carrying that signed buyer's order in your hand. In order for this to happen, you must be able to finalize the deal.

Throughout the entire sales process, you may have done everything right. You found the right car that fits your customer's wants and needs, and you established a relationship and built up the customer's trust and confidence in you. You may have even gotten a commitment from him or her to buy from you and progressed through the sales process overcoming countless objections the entire way; however, the customer will still not sign on the line.

It is time for the final step—the customer needs to sign on the line. Many people will realize that they have reached the end of the negotiation process, they have no more objections to be addressed, and they will finalize the deal. There are, however, a significant number of customers who hesitate to finalize their purchases by signing on the dotted line. They will regress. These are customers who need to be reassured that they are making the right decision, and you will need to find just the right words to set in motion the thoughts in your customers' minds that will convince them this is the right way for them to proceed. Your ability to provide this needed reassurance will ultimately determine how many sales you make versus how many sales you lose to your competitors.

This is the point where many salespeople seem to falter. Their best attempts at reassuring their customers and asking them to buy may go something like this. "What if I sold it to you for invoice? Would you buy it now?" one salesperson might say. Or another salesperson may ask, "What if I could get the payment down another ten or twenty dollars?" When there is no more money to give away and the deal is still not complete, these salespeople are forced to let their customer leave the dealership never knowing they could have closed the deal if they had just used a better approach to finalizing it.

The price may not even be the issue causing the customer to hesitate. More often than not, their minds are simply processing all of the information they have been given, and their own fears of making a mistake and the fear of the unknown are preventing them from making the final decision to buy.

It is all of the "what ifs" that are stopping them. The "what ifs" are uncontrollable factors your customer is wrestling with.

Examples

- What if I don't like the car after I have bought it?

- What if I can't handle the payment?

- What if I get laid off from work?

- What if I lose my job?

- What if gas prices go higher?

- What if one of the kids gets sick, and I have to pay high medical expenses?

These and similar questions bounce around inside of your customer's mind at that final moment of truth. Many times these questions are not even true objections—they are simply questions that your customer asks himself or herself out of fear. All of these possibilities existed when he or she decided to come to your dealership to buy a car in the first place, but now, at the moment of truth, these questions that are beyond anyone's control come to the forefront of the customer's mind.

It is easy to detect when you have reached this sticking point in the sales process. Your customer may become uneasy. Sometimes she will squirm in her seat; occasionally she will sit and stare off into space or at the worksheet containing the numbers. Another will look to her significant other as if to say, "Well, I can't make a decision, so it is up to you."

Many will follow this ritual by reusing one of the avoidances you learned about earlier in this book such as, "Well, I guess we just need to sleep on it," or, "We need to look at our budget again," and my favorite, "Well this is the first place we have looked." These are all typical responses. Why? Because you have come to a point where you are asking your customers to make a decision, and they know you have earned the right to ask for it. They feel obligated to you, but their fear of making a mistake is causing them to second-guess themselves. What they are really looking for at this point is guidance and reassurance.

They are looking for someone to tell them that buying this car is the right thing to do. In the rest of this chapter, I will share with you some of the ways you can be effective at reassuring your customers and guiding them past this sticking point.

Assume the Sale

As you have learned up to this point, each step of the sale is designed to gradually ease the customers into making one of the biggest purchasing decisions of their lives. You started with the basics; you found a car and educated them on it, proceeded to gain a commitment, contended with their objections, and followed through by negotiating the numbers. It seems only natural that you would expect them to complete the purchase. At this point, you must continue to be proactive. You cannot wait for the "what ifs" to take over the customers' thought processes. You cannot wait for them to decide that the safest thing to do would be to "look around some more" or "sleep on it." Your best defense against having to contend with the uncontrollable "what ifs" is a strong offense. You need to take the offensive position. Be proactive and assume the sale.

This sounds simple enough. However, I have seen many salespeople become their own roadblocks at this point. They see the customer pondering the finality of the deal, conjuring up all of the "what ifs," and they will sit there waiting, watching, and hoping that the customer does not go back on his or her commitment. This happens with such frequency that there is a common car business phrase for it. If you have ever heard someone say, "My customer is backing up," you know what I mean.

Customers have no problem "backing up" on the commitments they have given you. They may have signed their names to three different committed offers. However, if you pause at this critical time, the "what ifs" may kill your deal.

To help prevent this from happening, upon my return from the sales desk with an approved offer, I always exclaim, "Congratulations!" and offer my outstretched hand as I approach the table.

I am assuming that their committed offer is good and that they are buying the car. This also does two things; first, it sends the signal that the negotiations have ended, and second, it lets them and everyone around them know they have bought a car. Typically, this creates enough momentum in the sales process that it pushes them right past any second thoughts they may have. With just this one word, the customers can be mentally transported from the negotiating phase to the phase of ownership.

I conclude the sale by instructing them to provide me with the documentation I need to finish the deal. As they hand me these items (driver's licenses, registration to the trade, insurance card) that I had not gathered in previous phases of the sales process, they are coming to terms with the fact that they have purchased an automobile. They know they have finalized the deal.

Resell the Benefits

Assuming the sale is a great thing to do, and it would be wonderful if it worked every time. However, you will find that quite often your customers will need the reassurance I mentioned earlier. The most logical thing to do at this point is to resell the benefits and ask for their business again. Start by expressing empathy and proceed to highlight the attributes they expressed to be most important to them during the presentation and demonstration phase of the sales process. If reliability was what they expressed to you as the most important attribute about the car they wanted to purchase, then start by highlighting it, and continue by reminding them about the other features they showed interest in. If the customers loved the eight-way power adjustable seat, then bring that to their attentions. Conclude by assuring them that they are getting a great deal on the car, and ask them to buy again.

Example

Customer: I know I told you we were going to buy the car, but we really need to sleep on it.

Salesperson: I can understand your need to think about it. If I were buying a new car, I would probably be a little nervous too. However, I am just wondering if I missed something. You stated earlier that reliability was the most important aspect of the new vehicle you were going to purchase, and as you already know you're not going to get a more reliable vehicle than this one. Additionally, it has the bumper-to-bumper warranty for added piece of mind. This car seems to have all of the features you are looking for; it even has the eight-way power adjustable seat you liked so much. To top it all off, you know you are getting a fabulous deal. All I need to do is get a copy of both of your driver's licenses, and you can spend the rest of your day enjoying your new car.

Doing this helps to refresh the customers' memories on all of the reasons they should buy, rather than the reasons to be afraid of buying. Remember, once you have reached this point in the sale, all you are doing is trying to find creative ways to ask your customers to buy from you. If they have shopped at another store before yours, they have probably already passed on, "If I sell it to you for invoice, will you buy?" If they haven't shopped elsewhere, then you should at least try to finalize the deal without first giving away your paycheck.

Two Types of Buyers

It has been my experience that the people who are most apprehensive about finalizing a deal are the same customers who have been the most attentive to their true needs throughout the entire process. They did their homework before they came to your store, researching the cars they were interested in and possibly even comparing it with other models. While at your store, they took the time to look at more than one vehicle; they may have even test-driven several. During the negotiation process, they made every effort to stay within a predetermined budget. However, when it comes to finalizing the deal, they feel like they have missed something; they still want to think about it. If these customers leave your store, they normally "think about it" by going to another dealership and finding a salesman that is capable of closing a deal. To prevent this from happening, it is helpful to reassure them they have done everything possible to get the best deal on the vehicle that will suit their needs and, furthermore, is affordable with monthly payments that they can handle.

Example

Customer: I'm just not sure. I know I told you that I'd buy the car if you get to the payment I wanted, but I really need to think it over.

Salesperson: I can understand your need to think over such a purchase. In the years that I have been selling cars, I have typically seen that there are two types of buyers. One is the buyer that comes into the dealership on a whim with no forethought involved and jumps on the first vehicle they see. This person has an easy time making a decision but sometimes has a hard time paying for that decision. The second is the person, like yourself, that has done all of their homework, looked at all of their options, and found a car within their budget. They find it difficult to make that final decision, but once they have they don't have a problem paying for it. Now, why don't we get your car ready for delivery so you can take it home and start enjoying the new car you've earned?

Simple? Yes, it typically does not take any grand revelations for customers who are stuck on the verge of buying to be reassured they are making the right decision. If you are at this point in the sale, you should have already addressed their objections. Now you are only trying to keep the "what ifs" out of their minds and find another way to ask them to buy from you. The more ways you have of asking someone to buy from you, the better your chances are that they will.

If your attempts to reassure them fail, and your customer is still hiding behind the common avoidances we discussed in chapter eight, you may need to revert back to unmasking these avoidances and finding out what his or her objection is to buying now.

Joint Decision

Many times you will find yourself in front of a couple deciding to buy a car. You will reach that final moment, and the husband will look over at his wife, then stare at the worksheet in front of him, and then look back again at his wife. He is looking to her for reassurance, and she isn't giving it. Maybe she doesn't know that reassurance is what he is looking for. She doesn't know she can close the deal with only two words: "do it." Up until this point, he may have done all of the talking and may have seemed like the decision maker to you. However, the final say-so rests in the hands of his significant other because this decision, after all, is up to both of them. Remember from chapter seven, women influence 85 percent of all automotive-buying decisions.

I have found that if you let this situation play out, you normally end up hearing the dreaded, "We need to go talk about it first." If you realize early on that you are faced with these circumstances, you can often mediate the situation to a favorable resolution. You can finalize the deal and sell a car.

Example

Situation: You return from the sales desk with an approved offer and congratulate the couple on their purchase. The husband picks up the approved offer and stares at it without saying anything. He then looks at his wife as if to say, "Well what do you think? Should we do it?" He may even say those exact words. The wife offers no reassurance when she lays the decision squarely on his shoulders by saying, "It's up to you."

At this point, a stalemate has been reached. Neither party wants to make the final decision. Your best chance to finalize this sale is to mediate a resolution.

Husband: (Looks at figures, then back at wife)

Wife: (Either responds by not saying anything or by saying, "It's up to you.")

Salesperson: (To the wife) He's waiting for you to tell him it's OK with you. (Alternative response to the wife) I'm married too, and I know I wouldn't buy a car until my wife said it was OK. He is waiting for you to tell him it's OK. (Be sure to do this in a lighthearted manner and smile.)

Wife: (Typical response) It's OK with me, but it is his car.

Salesperson: (To husband) She said it's OK with her.

Wife: (At this point, the husband will typically look back at his wife.) It's OK with me. Just go ahead, and do it if you want to.

Husband: (Signs the buyer's order)

Addressing this subject can be a touchy situation. Surely it wouldn't play out the same way if the salesperson looked at the husband and said, "What are you waiting for, her permission?" when the husband looks at the wife for guidance. This is why it is important to choose your words carefully. It is even OK if you address the subject in a joking manner. All you are really doing is saying what the husband wants to say without making him say it in front of you. I have seen this scenario played out hundreds, if not thousands, of times, and I can assure you that when you address this subject with tact the very worst you will hear is, "We need to talk about it."

Need to Talk about It First

It would be a perfect business if there was one way of addressing every customer and every situation that would assure that you sold a car every time. This is not the case. Even after you have tried to intervene such as in the above example, there will still be times when one of the two looks at you and says, "We really need to talk about it first."

At this point, give them space. Stand up from the table, and tell them to take all the time they need. If you don't do this, you will be forcing them to discuss it somewhere else: at home or in their car on the way to another dealership. Neither scenario is good for you.

This may be a bit of a gamble, but it is much better than forcing your customers to leave. Maybe they really do need to discuss something without you present; maybe the wife wants her husband's reassurance that if they buy this car they will still be able to renovate the bathroom or the kitchen as they had agreed to do beforehand. Maybe there are private issues they need to discuss. The possibilities are endless; however, if you don't give them a chance to get these issues out in the open, they won't buy.

Once you have left the table, you will want to remain within sight but not towering over them. Typically, by the time you have gone to the sales desk and let the manager know what is going on (three to five minutes), they will have had time to discuss whatever it is that they needed to talk about but not enough time to have made a final decision on the purchase of the vehicle.

This is normally a good time to return to the table and assume the sale. You will find that returning to the table as if the customers have decided to buy and congratulating them may be a bit presumptuous, but you need to keep the momentum of the sale swinging in your direction even if their discussion wasn't favorable for you.

At this point, they will either buy from you, or they will at least know the reason they are holding off, and many times they will share it with you. Whatever the reason is, at least now you have an objection to address.

Remember, just as no two people are exactly alike, no two car deals are alike. Many of the examples given in this and previous chapters are based on the most common situations you will encounter and the most effective ways to proceed when you encounter them. When I initially set out to write this book, I planned to include everything a person could ever learn about selling cars in one book. However, the more I wrote, the more I realized it was impossible to include everything in only one book. Not only was it impossible, but it was ridiculous for me to believe that it was possible. Selling cars is about human interaction. It is about continually learning, continually adapting, and never thinking you know everything there is to know about the subject. Every customer you meet and every deal you work will be a new adventure.

The salespeople I have met who have the most success in their careers all have one common trait—consistency. They find something that works for them, and they do it over and over. They treat all of their customers with respect. They don't forget about the people that they have sold and that have helped get them to where they are now. Furthermore, none of the truly successful salespeople I have met sit back and rest on the work they have done in the past. They consistently look to improve and find new business.

CHAPTER THIRTEEN
FOLLOWING UP AND PROSPECTING

"Most of us never recognize opportunity until it goes to work in our competitor's business."

—P. L. Andarr

Up to this point, everything in this book has focused on increasing your chances of selling a car to the customer in front of you. If you are fortunate enough to have a continuous, never-ending flow of potential buyers streaming in to see you, then you will find the information in this chapter unnecessary. I do not think, however, that many of you find yourself in this position. It is for this reason that your ability to follow up with your customers and prospect for new ones is crucial to transforming your job selling cars, living from paycheck to paycheck, into a successful, stable career as an automotive sales professional.

Sure, making phone calls to potential and existing customers or writing thank-you notes and sending out birthday cards is not as instantly gratifying as sitting in front of a customer working a deal; nor is prospecting for new clientele. As salespeople, most of us love to be "in the moment." By that I mean we love to be head-to-head, one-on-one, with our customers while trying to instantly increase the size of our paychecks. In this business, as in life, you will find that if you live only for the moment, you may not have much of a future.

Following Up

As the saying goes, "You reap what you sow." This is also true regarding the automobile business. If you give consistent effort to keep your name in the minds of your customers, letting them know from the time they become a prospect and then continuously thereafter once they have purchased a vehicle from you that you want to be the one they buy all of their cars from, then you will enjoy the benefits and rewards that come with it. On the other hand, if you don't take time to plant these seeds and nurture your customer database, you will always find yourself standing on the front porch trying to outrun the four newest salespeople on the floor.

Sounds ridiculous, doesn't it? Could a salesperson really spend two hours with a prospect and never write a follow up letter or place a call to them? Could they be so foolish as to sell a vehicle and not even send the customer a thank-you note or call periodi cally to check on them? These questions are answered each time a customer walks in the door of the showroom and states, "I bought a car from here a year ago, but I don't remember my salesman's name." Or even worse, "I was in here three days ago and worked with a salesman, but I can't remember his name." Yes, it is possible that salespeople today still survive in a business as competitive as the automotive-sales industry without dedicat ing themselves to a consistent practice of follow up. Hopefully, though, you are looking for more than a way to survive.

Nowadays, it is easier than ever to formulate and follow through with an effective plan for follow-up with your custom ers and potential clients. With advancements in technology, you are afforded the luxury of being able to collect information on your customer, enter it into a computer, and implement a regi mented follow-up plan that will take less time out of your day than most salespeople take figuring out what to order for lunch. "Computer? What computer?" you may be asking yourself. If you are, then unfortunately you are one of those people whom the information age has passed by. Get with the times. Work smarter, not harder. Invest the amount of one good commission on the price of a new computer, and use this tool to give your self a pay raise for years to come.

However you decide to manage your customers' information is your choice. Regardless of the method you use, the important part is that you use it. Many salespeople do not maximize the potential of the information available to them. Typically, they meet a customer, sell him or her a car, and then maybe send a thank-you note. Well, that is a start, but it is doubtful that the one thank-you note you sent will ensure that your customer remembers your name when he or she decides to buy another car or to refer a friend or family member to your dealership. You have to keep your name in front of the customer on a continual basis. After all, famous people are even forgotten by the public if their names are not kept in the limelight. Here are just a few examples of opportunities that you have to keep your name in front of your customers.

Examples

Call Immediately

Call and leave a message on your customer's home phone thanking them for the opportunity to do business or for buying from you the moment they depart your store.

Send a Thank-You Note Immediately

Send a short note thanking your customers for their purchase or for the opportunity you had to earn their business that day if they did not buy from you.

Call Daily

Call the customers who have the most potential of buying from you in the very near future at least once a day, if not more. Most people today have cell phones and can be reached anywhere. Be sure to get this number and use it. Don't be afraid to call your prospective customers. Don't be bashful. Remember the words that were said to me by a thirty-year, forty-car-a-month veteran salesman as he stepped in front of me to wait on a customer that I was preparing to greet, "A bashful beggar always has an empty purse."

Send Cards on Special Occasions

Your customers' birthdays or anniversaries may not seem like a time for you to celebrate. However, for them these are some of the most important days in their lives. If they receive a card from you, it will only strengthen their belief that you not only care about their business but also about them. Some of your customers may not receive a card from certain family members on their special day, but if they receive one from you, they will remember you. After all, you remembered them on their special day.

- **Birthdays**
- **Wedding anniversaries**
- **Holidays**
- **On the anniversary of their purchase from you**

Send Letters Whenever Possible

If your store has a big sale coming up, be sure to notify all of your current customers. Yes, even the ones you sold recently. Let them know that if they are in need of another new car, or if they happen to have a friend or family member in the market for a vehicle, there is no better time than the present to send them in to see you.

Call Frequently

Many salespeople conveniently forget to call their customers every few months or so to see how they are doing with their new vehicles. Maybe they are afraid that a customer will voice a concern. This is the exact reason you need to call. If you are there for your customers when they have questions or concerns about their vehicles, then you can be proactive in making sure they remain happy. If necessary, involve yourself in having their vehicles serviced. Set their appointments in the service department for them. Greet them when they arrive at your store for service. Show your customers that you didn't forget them, and they will not forget you.

Get E-mail Addresses

All of the big companies have gotten on the bandwagon. Anytime you contact representatives of a major corporation, they want your e-mail address. Why? Because they know this is an inexpensive and effective way to get their company in front of consumers. Much like these companies, you too are in business for yourself, so if you haven't started using e-mail to reach your customers, ask yourself why not? E-mail is not a technology reserved only for the Internet sales department in your dealership. It is another means for you to stay in touch with your customers and to keep your name fresh in their memories. In case you didn't know, as of the year 2000 the census bureau reported on www.census.gov that more than 40 percent of the households in America have an Internet-connected computer, and the first thing most people do when they get on their computer is check their e-mail.

You may even want to consider starting your own e-mail-delivered newsletter. You can keep your customers updated on new vehicles that will be released; specials that your sales, parts, and service departments are running; and even personal news about the great things that have been happening for you lately. Have you been recognized by your dealership as salesperson of the month or of the year? Have you recently become factory certified or been presented with an award from the manufacturer? If so, you can include all of these things in your e-mail newsletter.

To do this though, you must first get your customers' e-mail addresses. Customers don't offer it to you for no reason. To get it, all you need to do is ask for it. Most people you talk to will be happy to give you their e-mail addresses when you explain that you will notify them of any upcoming events that will save them money. Imagine the number of e-mail addresses you could gather if you obtained one from only 50 percent of the customers you talked to on the phone or in person. If you talk to an average of three customers each day, then you should add approximately five hundred e-mail addresses per year to your list. Now you have the ability to contact these five hundred people with the click of a mouse. In five years, you would have more than twenty-five hundred customers whom you could contact any time you felt like selling a car, and the only cost to you would be your time.

"A wise man will make more opportunities than he finds."

—Francis Bacon

Create New Ways

When it comes to keeping your name in the forefront of your customers' minds, the possibilities are endless. So far, we have examined only a few of the most common methods. If you use your imagination, you will find there are more ways you haven't thought of than the number of ways you have.

For example, you might want to consider having stickers made with your name, place of business, and phone number that you can stick to the door jamb of every car you sell. Most customers won't mind. After all, your dealership probably places its logo directly on the trunk lid of their new vehicles anyway. Show your customers where you placed your information (not that most of them wouldn't see it every time they open the car door anyway). Inform them you placed it there so that they know who to call if they ever have a problem. Your customers will surely remember your name if they see it every time they get in and out of their vehicles.

If investing in stickers is a little too expensive for you to do at this time, get some clear packing tape and tape your business card in the door jamb. This sure beats putting it in with the owner's manual, a place where your customers only go when they are replacing their old registration with the new one.

Keep in mind that repeat and referral business is the easiest, most lucrative business you will have in your career. Without it, you won't have a career—you will only have a job.

Prospecting

On January 24, 1848, James W. Marshall discovered gold at Sutter's Mill. This single discovery touched off one of the greatest migrations in the history of the United States. It is commonly referred to as the California Gold Rush. Tens of thousands of people risked their lives to migrate across the country in hopes of finding a fortune hidden beneath the hills and in the rivers of the great Wild West.

Different from the prospectors of the gold rush era, you, as a salesperson, don't need to risk your life or travel three thousand miles to discover wealth beyond your wildest dreams. You are surrounded by your most precious resource right where you are now. Whether you live in a small town in the Midwest or in a major city in the Northeast, your potential customers—resources as valuable as gold—are all around you. All you need to do is prospect for them. How much of this resource do you encounter on a daily basis and yet never realize its value?

The average person in the United States interacts with twenty to twenty-five people each day. As a car salesman, ten to fifteen of the people you interact with may be other car salesman or sales managers. However, that still leaves five to ten people you interact with each day that could be potential customers. Ask yourself, out of these five to ten people that you interact with on a daily basis, how many of them know where you work, what you do for a living, or even your name? If these people don't know all of this information about you, then chances are the first time you will hear them discussing their automotive needs is when they are bragging about the good deal they just got on the new vehicle that they have already purchased.

As I mentioned earlier in this chapter, "a bashful beggar has an empty purse." You can't be shy and successful at selling cars simultaneously. Assume that everyone you encounter is in the market for a new car. Whether you are at the grocery store paying for your groceries, talking to a waiter or waitress at a restaurant, or even standing in line at the bank discussing the weather with a complete stranger, make sure to let others know who you are. Tell them what you do for a living and emphasize the fact that you would like them to come see you when they are considering an automobile purchase. Practice the art of shameless self-promotion.

Additionally, you should try to increase the number of people you come in contact with on a daily basis. Remember, I said the average person interacts with twenty to twenty-five people each day. Most people buying a book such as the one you are holding didn't do so just to become average. Furthermore, most people who decide to sell cars and earn an above-average income, decided to do so because they wanted to earn more than the average person. If you want to be above average, you need to increase the number of people you interact with on a daily basis. Participate in community events; join local clubs, teams, and organizations. If you increase the number of people you are exposed to on a daily basis and make sure they all know who you are, what you do for a living, and that you want to be the person they buy their next car from, you will generate new business for yourself and your dealership.

To some reading this chapter, the points I am making may seem elementary, and the reason for this is because they are. These points are the basic fundamentals of prospecting for new customers. Why then, if these fundamentals are so basic, does the typical car salesperson consume less than one box of business cards in a year? The answer is easy—because they don't prospect.

Remember from chapter one, the difference between being a salesperson and performing any other job in the world is that a salesperson does not get paid until he or she generates revenue. Furthermore, the more revenue you generate, the more money you will earn. Prospecting for new customers is the backbone to your success at generating more revenue than your peers. Anyone with a pulse can stand on the front porch of a dealership and wait for a customer to show up. It takes a real salesperson to make sure that the customers who are pulling onto your lot are asking for you. Become aware of your opportunities to create new business for yourself and utilize them to their maximum potential. Below are only a few examples of ways you can prospect for new business.

"The sure way to miss success is to miss the opportunity."

—Victor Charles

Examples

Use your business cards.

As a salesperson, your business card is your billboard. Don't be afraid to use it. It is not just for the prospects that come into your dealership. Business cards are for anyone with whom you come in contact. Give them to the waiters and waitresses you meet at the restaurants where you dine. Give them to the teller at the bank where your checks are deposited. Give them to the cashier at the convenience store who takes your money for a purchase. Give them to your neighbors. Give them to the person who delivers your mail. Give them to the men picking up your garbage. Remember, no one you meet is under qualified to receive your business card. When people see you coming, you want them to think, "Here comes John. He will probably give me another one of his business cards." This may seem a little corny, but the next time they are in the market for a new vehicle, they will know your name, and they will know that you want their business.

Put your business cards to work for you.

You may be at your dealership every hour that the doors are open, but that doesn't mean that the minute the store closes the customers stop coming to look. Whether it is on a Sunday morning or in the middle of the night, customers will come to look at the vehicles that your dealership has for sale. It doesn't matter to them whether the doors to your dealership are open or closed; all they know is that they need a change. They need a new vehicle.

It would be nice if you could be at the store twenty-four hours a day, seven days a week. However, since you can't, you need to put your business cards to work for you. Place them on the windshield of every vehicle on the lot before you leave each night. The minute one of these after-hours shoppers finds a car they are interested in, they instinctively will grab your card and stick it in their pocket. Why? Because they will have questions they need answered, and guess who they are going to ask for when they call to get those questions answered? That's right, you.

Treat everyone like they bought from you.

Just because potential customers didn't buy from you the first time you met them doesn't mean they never will. Maybe they bought somewhere else this time just because they got more for their trade-in at the other dealership. Maybe the other dealership just had a vehicle that suited their needs better. Maybe they just didn't realize the value of the relationship you were trying to build with them. Whatever the reason they did not buy from you this time, this should bear no significance to the relationship that you have begun with this couple. Treat them like they are your customers and like they bought a car from you, even if they didn't. After all, if you treat everyone you meet like they are already your customers, then you will increase the chances of them actually becoming one.

Keep in touch with them. Send them cards, letters, and e-mail. You may even want to call them periodically to let them know that you remember them and would like a chance to earn their business the next time they are in the market. By doing these things, you will keep your name fresh in their minds in case the need arises for them to make another change. Remember, twenty-first century families have need for more than one car. Furthermore, the average trade cycle of two to three years is a short time in comparison to the length of your career. Consider this: they probably haven't heard from "what's his name" who sold them their last car since they drove off the lot two years ago.

"When one door closes another door opens; but we often look so long and so regretfully upon the closed door that we do not see the ones which open for us."

— Alexander Graham Bell

Ask for referrals.

People love to talk about their cars and how they bought them. Whether you are in a grocery store or at a car wash, you will frequently overhear people talking about either the great deal they just got on their new car or the need they have for a new one. Americans love cars, and they love to talk about them.

For this reason, the customers you have sold can be your biggest advocates and your best sources of new business; so let them know that you want them to be advocates. Tell them every chance you get that you want them to send you their friends, their family members, and anyone they talk to who has an interest in buying a car. Let them know that you want them to talk about you.

Remember that the customers who have purchased from you have already expressed the fact that they like the way you do business. They expressed this sentiment when they signed the purchase order, solidifying their own purchases. Because of this, they can be your best advertisement. The key words in that last sentence are "can be." If you don't ask them for referrals, you will one day fall victim to the fated words, "Yeah, I sent my friend over to buy a car at your dealership, but I didn't want to bother you," from one of your previous customers.

When it comes to prospecting for new business, the opportunities available to you are only limited by your imagination and by your motivation to pursue them. The choice you need to make is whether you want to give the extra effort needed to establish a stable, lucrative career or whether you will be happy knowing that twenty years from now, if you survive in the business that long, you will still be standing on the front porch, waiting to outrun the new guy so that you can get to the customer pulling on the lot. *You decide.*

Afterword

It has been nearly two decades since I sat in on my first Saturday-morning sales meeting. With my adrenaline pumping, fueled purely by my inspiration and unbridled desire, I could only imagine the possibilities that the car business held for me. Still, almost twenty years later, I remember the feeling as if I'd had it yesterday. Why? Because I still get that feeling. I get it every morning when I climb out of bed and get ready to go to work, all the while knowing that I work in the car business—a business that will allow me to grow to my full potential. You see, the car business does not have limits. It has endless and undiscriminating opportunities limited only by one's desire and willingness to meet its never-ending challenges. The great ones thrive off of these challenges. They even seek them out. Hopefully, you are one of these people.

The business of selling cars is one of the most honest, yet least forgiving that there is. Each week you get a good look at yourself in the mirror. You get this candid look at the value of the work you do when you open the envelope containing your paycheck. As you will see, selling cars can be the easiest low-paying job you will ever have. Or, if you have the heart of a lion and are driven to succeed, it will be the highest-paying hard work you have ever performed.

While the car business is a never-ending process of discovering your own strengths, acknowledging your weaknesses, and pushing your limits to become just a little better than you were the day before, it is your ability to use the tools you have been given within these pages that will determine how fast you climb to the top. You must strive to perfect the art of their use in any situation and with any customer. You must also take control of your own attitude and become the master of it. Finally, you must put your enthusiasm to work for you in your attempt to inspire the people with whom you come in contact.

Learn more about selling cars at

www.Showroomtoday.com

The Spot for Automotive Sales Professionals

You can contact Jeffrey F. Knott by sending e-mail to:

Jeff@ShowroomToday.com

Bibliography

The Forbes Book of Business Quotations. New York: Black Dog and Leventhal Publishers, 1997.

Gunnell, John. *100 Years of American Cars.* Lola, WI: Krause Publications, 1993.

Hall, Edward. *The Hidden Dimension.* New York: Anchor Books, 1982.

Koch, Richard. *The 80/20 Principle: The Secret to Success by Achieving More with Less.* New York: Doubleday, 1998.

978-1-58348-019-9
1-58348-019-6